Arthur Brisbane's

KAN SAS CITY

by
Kansas City Times columnist
Arthur S. Brisbane

Rosalindajones
Enterprises Inc.

To Jo

ACKNOWLEDGMENT

The author gratefully acknowledges permission to reprint material from *The Kansas City Times,* published by the Kansas City Star Company, 1729 Grand Ave., Kansas City, Mo. 64108.

ILLUSTRATIONS

CONTENTS

CHAPTER 6 THE SPORTING LIFE

CHAPTER 7 NO BUSINESS LIKE SHOW BUSINESS

CHAPTER 8 CAFE KANSAS CITY

CHAPTER 9 GOING TO EXTREMES

CHAPTER 10 HIGH ANXIETY

LIVING
THE GOOD
LIFE

Spot
made his move to
Wealth

Concerning Spot, a dog whose rags-to-riches story should be an inspiration to right-thinking Americans. Or . . . how a mutt got wise and declared his independence.

Spot is one of those dogs who looks as if he were manufactured during the shift break at the dog factory. The parts don't fit. One ear stands cocked, the other lies flat.

The colors don't match properly either. Spot's head is mostly collie, with the appropriate shades of brown, white and gold. The rest of him is primarily white with small, dark spots. Hence the name Spot, a dog.

Spot's physical uniqueness, however, is not his most important aspect. It is his personality that stands out. He is extraordinarily nice. Very pleasant to be around.

The factory would never recall Spot for a character defect. He is pure dog: loyal, loving, friendly. He gets along with other dogs and all but the most obnoxious human beings. He obeys, for the most part.

As befits his good character and manners, Spot currently resides in a rather elegant home along Ward Parkway. In Kansas City, only the best live on Ward Parkway.

Spot has the run of the beautifully decorated interior of his owner's house. He can romp outdoors near the patio or the pool or in the yard. Spot can do as he pleases now, because he a dog of leisure.

If he wanted to, Spot could take out one of those ads that say, "How I found financial independence in my spare time." His picture would run with the ad. He would be chewing a massive steak bone, smiling with one ear cocked.

But Spot, being a dog and a modest one at that, would be unlikely to do such a thing. He'll probably just live out his days in quiet bliss.

He's earned it. Life, you must understand, hasn't always been a bed of roses for Spot, a dog.

When he arrived on the Ward Parkway doorstep, Spot was a mess. He was frightened, underfed and had quite obviously been beaten, more than likely by some obnoxious human being. Spot was on the lam.

His present owner took one look at the ratty, bony, beaten creature and felt great pity. There was already one dog in the house, but this spotted fellow with the collie head needed help right away.

Spot received food and shelter. The Ward Parkway resident did all the other appropriate things nice human beings do when they take in dogs on the lam.

The new owner called the Lost Dog Registry. But the registry knew nothing of Spot. The owner took Spot to a veterinarian, who examined him and concluded, "He certainly shouldn't go back to where he came from."

Where had Spot come from? His new owner was curious. In the ensuing months, as Spot adjusted to his new home, there was no clue. Spot never once mentioned his past.

The mystery was finally explained by a carpet layer. The carpet layer, while hard at work improving Spot's home, drew close to the dog and had a good look at him. Then he asked Spot's owner, "Where did you get this dog?"

The owner explained that Spot's origins were unknown.

"I've seen that dog somewhere before," the carpet layer said. "On Prospect Street, guarding a used-car lot."

Then the carpet layer added more details of Spot's past. The dog had been stationed in the middle of the lot, chained and charged with the responsibility of warding off would-be thieves.

Presumably, the other telltale signs of Spot's former life — the beat marks, the undernourishment — could be attributed to his job at the car lot.

Suddenly, it all came clear to Spot's new owner. Spot had taken that job and shoved it. The food was lousy, what little there was of it. And the boss was apparently an obnoxious human being. So the dog broke the shackles of his unfortunate condition.

How Spot got from the car lot on Prospect to his oasis on Ward Parkway remains unknown. But it certainly was a smart move for a dog. It was a move that many human beings, as hard as they might try, have been unable to make.

Spot could have settled down somewhere along Main Street or Wornall Road. Those are pretty fair neighborhoods. But this canine Horatio Alger character went all the way. He went to Ward Parkway.

So that's the rags-to-riches story of Spot, a dog. It will never be known precisely how he managed to climb the social ladder so high, or what moral and sociological lessons lie therein.

It can only be said that Spot is happy now.

"Woof."

Isn't it all "**Just Great**" at the ball?

OK, so you're not debutante material. You could never make it as an escort. You're a slob, and everybody knows it. But that doesn't mean you can't go to the city's elegant Jewel Ball next week.

Sure, you'll have to crash it. But once inside, with the right look, the right conversation, the right *je ne sais quoi,* you'll fit in where the fitting counts.

You've never considered going to the Jewel Ball, you say? That's understandable. Every year this festive event passes in a blaze of hoopla, and only the very best people get to go. The slobs pass that Friday night in a blaze of barbecue and beer.

It's an age-old story really. High society wouldn't be very high without a low society to compare itself with.

Class distinctions should have been wiped out with the American Revolution. They weren't, of course, but where's the law that says you can't dream? Just picture yourself: soft lights, a dance band playing "Just One of Those Things," an aristocratic member of the opposite sex melting in the magic of your conversation . . .

Yes, dreamer, it could happen to you. But you'll need to prepare yourself. You'll need to handle yourself just so. You'll need a lot of money for clothes.

As far as I know, there is no used debutante clothing store in Kansas City. So, sell your car and buy a nice gown. Stay away from sharp colors and patterns. You're trying to look elegant, not loud.

If you're a male, you can rent a tuxedo for less than a hundred dollars, so you probably won't need to sell your car. Stick with a black suit, because the lighter colors will make you look like a conventioneer.

In the week that remains before the June 26 gala, you should practice your conversational skills. These are most essential because a genuine Jewel Ball guest will be able to pick up on the slightest sign of low-class conversational skills. If this happens, you'll be thrown out of the ball and will have to go back to being a slob.

These high-class conversational skills are not difficult to master. You won't need to know much about international politics or literary matters. You can talk about the Royals if you want. It's all in *how* you talk.

Master these easy adjectives: "marvelous," "divine," "just great" and "really great." Say the words slowly, and stretch out the vowels until your cheeks hurt.

In almost any conversation you're likely to have at the Jewel Ball, you can always fall back on these high-class adjectives. Imagine a scenario: You've managed to sneak past the reception desk in your newly acquired finery, and someone asks you what school you went to.

"Pem Day?"

What do you say — "No, Raytown South"? Of course not. You simply gesture expansively, smile as widely as you can and say something like, "Oh, yes, yes, just great. Isn't this simply divine?"

Such remarks at debutante parties are almost always greeted with smiles and a series of echoing remarks. At the Jewel Ball, you can be safely assured "marvelous" will get you a drink, all the hors d'oeuvres you want and even a turn or two on the floor.

But be advised: You should direct your conversation to the older generation. They are held in thrall by this event and are much more likely to be taken in.

Parents of debutantes are convinced that their children are "coming out," a process that the parents perceive through an emotional haze but that, roughly translated, means the children have ditched their jeans for the night and agreed to "come out" in gowns and tuxedos. Some of the debutantes and escorts, you will discover, would rather be in a Kansas beer joint.

When talking with the parents, therefore, always refer to how "divine" the young are looking tonight.

If someone should attempt to draw you out in a discussion of golf or hog futures, or some other substantive topic, there are easy ways to extricate yourself before anybody figures out that you're a slob and shouldn't be at the Jewel Ball.

Don't panic. Keep that smile crisp and wide. Take a sip from your drink. Then, just as you start to say, "I've put some thought into that lately," look to the side suddenly and say: "Why, it's old Elliott! Great guy! Haven't seen him since Pem Day. Excuse me, won't you? Marvelous."

Sound easy? Well it is. A slob like you can scale the heights of society by following a few simple instructions. Just remember: At the Jewel Ball, everyone is divine, and you will be too.

Dodo
beat the odds with
Life

He was a little fellow, just 4 feet 8 inches tall, and so his clothes had to be custom-made by his sister-in-law. His head was oversized, his face too flat. He couldn't talk very well and tended to answer, "I did, I did," when a question was put to him.

But when Milford Earl "Dodo" Bevelle was laid to rest Wednesday he wasn't lacking for friends to witness it.

Dodo, as he had been known since his early years, was a neighborhood fixture on Kansas City's West Side. He mixed with youngsters and adults. He played on the ball fields and walked his dog. He rode the city's streetcar and bus lines. Later in life he made regular appearances in taverns, although he never drank.

He did a lot of things that ordinary people do. But Dodo Bevelle was never ordinary.

According to the odds back in 1919, the year he was born, Dodo should have been shunned by society, perhaps even hidden away in a closet or institution somewhere. He should have died before the age of 20.

He was born with Down's syndrome, also known as Mongolism. Life back then was brutish and short for anyone who suffered its debilitating physical symptoms and mental retardation. Down's syndrome sufferers used to die young of heart problems, neglect and ignorance — other people's ignorance mostly.

But Dodo Bevelle never was shunned. He was accepted, indeed embraced, by the neighborhood where he was reared. He lived to be 62.

"I never realized he was so old," said attorney William Ergovich, a friend who attended the funeral. "But, of course, you thought of him as a child."

Dodo was the last of eight born to Rhoda Bevelle, who was 45 when he came into the world. Mrs. Bevelle believed in treating Dodo like all the rest, even though he couldn't go to school.

When Mrs. Bevelle herself was ready to enter a nursing home late in life she told her son Billy: "Don't ever put him in a home. Take care of him."

Billy Bevelle always had taken care of him. The two were inseparable on the West Side, where neighborhood activity centered on Mulkey Park, or "Monkey Park," as the kids preferred to call it. There Dodo learned to play softball.

It was characteristic of him, right through middle age, to be seen hanging around the park holding a gunnysack filled with softball equipment. The bats and balls were a source of influence for Dodo.

"If you didn't want to play by his rules, he'd take his bag and leave," Billy Bevelle said.

John "Rube" Ruby, a retired bar owner, recalled the time Dodo wanted to pitch: "Well, Dodo couldn't pitch, but he had all the equipment. So he pitched. They scored 23 runs off him in the first inning, and we tried to pull him. But he said no."

That's the way it was. Dodo Bevelle was different, yet he was a part of the close-knit neighborhood. People made allowances for him.

As an adult Dodo lived outside the mainstream of life. He had no job. He roamed the city. Nevertheless, he established a consistent routine.

He could be found hanging around 12th Street, where he walked a regular circuit. He could be found riding the streetcars or buses, often for free because the drivers knew him.

Or he could be found in the company of children. It seemed that children always had a special fondness for him.

"Not a one of those kids thought he was dumb or crazy," Billy Bevelle said. "But the older people thought that sometimes. People would stare. That's why I think you have to keep people like Dodo out in the open — then more people would accept them."

Dodo was always out in the open. Staying alternately with his sister Irene and brother Billy, he had the run of the city. It got him into trouble once.

Somebody pulled a false alarm at a Downtown theater, and when the Fire Department arrived Dodo was asked who did it. He answered: "I did, I did." Dodo told the same thing to the judge and was sentenced to 30 days on the municipal farm.

Friends intervened. Dodo faced another judge. This time he changed his testimony and soberly shook his head "no."

As the years rolled by, family and friends increasingly were mystified by Dodo's longevity. People would see Dodo with Billy Bevelle and his wife, Margaret, and ask: "Is that Dodo from the West Side? Is he still alive?"

What kept Dodo Bevelle going?

Doctors said it was regular exercise. But Billy Bevelle thinks that it was love that kept Dodo going. Love, and the chance to live among people, to be a part of the world and not a refugee from it.

A
Free
spirit adapting to
Society

It's been tough to keep a stiff upper lip in Kansas City since Kate Kemper's arrival two years ago.

Kate, the daughter of *New Yorker* magazine critic Brendan Gill, married R. Crosby Kemper III, scion of the city's most prominent banking family. When Crosby III brought home the bride it was quickly apparent that she was not going to be your typical banker's wife.

Kate, who tells colorful stories with gusto and much gesturing, soon had local society matrons biting their tongues at the dinner table. With a loquacious style learned as one of seven children in a talkative family, Kate entertains with a verve perhaps better suited to literary types in tweed than businessmen in pin stripes.

Stories abound of her puckish humor, her delight in slapstick. But they are stories Kate no longer particularly likes to hear about herself.

There was a time at a wedding held at the Kansas City Club when Kate took the floor and sang her rendition of a little known classic, "Skin Tango."

Then there was the time, at the end of her brief career as a fund-raiser for former Mayor Charles B. Wheeler, when Kate was heard singing in the corridors of the 29th floor of the City Hall. The occasion was Wheeler's last day in office and Kate explained, "I started singing because this was the day the passion died."

Kate's friends note that, just for laughs, she sometimes likes to take people's words literally. (Sort of like the Marx Brothers joke: "If you sit on my right hand and you sit on my left, what am I going to eat with?") At a local restaurant, a waitress asked Kate and a friend, "Would you like onions with your sandwiches?"

"No," they responded.

"Well, if you do later on, just holler," the waitress offered. Later on, they were heard hollering, "Onions! Onions!"

By this time, most society matrons have learned that if they want this banker's wife to serve on the board of this or that, they'd better prepare themselves for the unpredictable.

'' 'Well, you certainly are refreshing,' they would say," Kate recalls.

"Then after the fifth visit, it was 'Oh, my God!' "

Kate is repentant now. "I don't want to be off anybody's dance card," she says.

After two years of slapstick in Kansas City society, she's beginning to realize that a few adjustments must be made. But it's hard for her to fit in. "As far as Kansas City is concerned, the honeymoon is over," she says.

Can Kate Kemper find happiness without singing in the rain? Ah, that is a good question.

A faint look of remorse crosses her face as Kate ponders the difficulty of blending her style with the Establishment style of Kansas City's Kempers. It is a rare and tranquil moment for a face that usually is struggling to keep up with her rapid-fire conversation.

At 28, Kate clearly shares some of the facial features of her famous father — dark hair and prominent eyebrows and nose. She is tall and substantial and her entrance into a room rarely goes unnoticed. Kate makes few concessions to the latest fashion, either in her dress or in the decor of the home she shares with her husband.

She recalls that when she arrived here, she was met with open arms by the Kemper clan. The rest of high society here, she says, greeted her with great generosity. But, "given an inch, I took a mile. And the mile is what I regret."

It's easy to understand why Kate's background made things difficult here. The sixth of seven children, she grew up in an old Victorian home in Bronxville, N.Y., a suburb of New York City.

Her family encouraged all types of dramatic productions by the children at home. Kate recalls occasionally going to school in pajama tops and blue jeans and enjoying the rough and tumble life of a tomboy.

"They would always say, 'Oh, here comes a Gill.' We were a great family but slightly weird."

It was after her graduation from high school that Kate took a fateful trans-Atlantic cruise for a year's study abroad. She met Crosby III on the boat and, as she describes it, they were opposite personalities drawn together. She was unnerved.

"If anybody saw me with the guy my reputation as a liberal would be ruined," she remembers, not really kidding. "He was a right-winger, a John Wayne aficionado."

Although the romance flickered off for a while, they got together again and were married after college. Then it was off to Kansas City to be a banker's wife.

"I didn't believe in banks," she says. "I never went to banks. When we needed money, we just called the mysterious Uncle Louie. Now I am a hardy believer in banks. I am hip to large margins and short-term loans."

These days Kate does some free-lance writing (she has a book review column in *City* magazine) and spends the rest of her time in the miscellaneous pursuit of everything from philosophical truth to mayonnaise sandwiches.

"Each day I feel an increasing fitness to live," she says, quoting Henry James and wondering whether she'll *ever* master the Kemper style.

'69
grads dance to
Memories

It was their 10th reunion.

Like any class returning to see itself, the Class of '69 at Shawnee Mission East High School stumbled into the banquet hall all agog, eyes searching for a familiar face, hands reaching for a drink.

They came well dressed, mostly, except for the class characters who stayed true to form and arrived in track shoes, leather jackets and low-cut dresses. Some wore massive doses of rouge; others displayed their watch fobs.

They had not changed that much. They looked prosperous.

Shawnee Mission East — in the class of '69 there had been no blacks and few whom could be called poor. With the rest of American youth in that year, these affluent Johnson County offspring had rambled leftward.

In their senior year the spirit of protest brought down the dress code, brought in the smell of dope and sent a generation of parents scurrying for cover. By Memorial Day weekend 1979, however, the class of '69 was back in the middle of the road.

Why had they come back? They were curious, for one thing.

What could possibly have happened to the girl who departed early, pregnant and on her way to the altar? Answer: She's divorced, with plenty of company in the class of '69.

And did you hear about Sandahl Bergman, the "most talented" girl in the class, now a singing and dancing star on Broadway?

Could Peggy Schiffman ever have known she would end up selling anti-pollution devices to heavy industry?

They came to assess themselves, to measure one another's progress through adulthood. The values of adolescence had made sense on graduation day. But in the intervening years, things changed.

It was not so important anymore to have played the fool in class, or to have dated the campus queen. Gone were the days when personal worth could be gauged by whether a person was wise enough to lunch at Winstead's on the Plaza.

In those days it was of consequence to know that to be "correct" one had to park at that restaurant only in certain spaces, and always to back the car in.

But now professional goals, marriage, financial security and, in some cases, the urge to get far away transfixed the class of '69. Gathered in the lobby, they talked about themselves.

"Everything's going great," one man announced. "I'm living in Overland Park and I'm in the junk business. It's a family thing, you know. But it's a good business. Meet my wife, Julia. She's expecting in October." Julia looked shyly on, a victim of someone else's reunion.

Across the room a svelte grad in a sheer dress, labeled a "loose woman" in high school, talked about her young child born out of wedlock. But instead of reproving glances from her classmates, she heard, "You know, it really looks like you were ahead of your time."

For every person whose mischievous smile hadn't changed an iota, there was the surprise graduate. Johnny Rowlands, for example. In school he was quiet, hardly the sort to attract much attention. So where, as the cliche goes, is he now?

Now he's got such a big mouth they decided to give him a microphone. He's one of the premier disc jockeys for radio station KBEQ, a heartthrob to the teen-age girls who listen to the station.

While some, like Johnny Rowlands and Sandahl Bergman, loomed large as well-known graduates, others used the reunion to advertise their budding careers. A reunion provides a forum for vanity, and vanity breeds gossip.

As the alumni filed into the banquet hall — nearly 300 out of 681 had shown up — they got an eyeful of a man who's made vanity his profession.

There, tacked on a bulletin board along with snapshots of other classmates, was an 8x10 glossy photo sent in by Don Murray, who had journeyed to Hollywood for a career as an actor and producer.

Staring out from the black and white, Murray looked back at his class in silent testimony to the dry look. The picture drew not a few snickers.

What had started as a loose congregation of familiar faces coalesced after dinner around John Gage, the old class president recently graduated from law school. Gage stepped nervously to the mike and began the proceedings with, "Hyuk, I was never too good at this in high school either."

Gage presented the usual reunion awards for the wildest and craziest, the most-traveled, the most helpful reunion worker and the most foul-mouthed.

Then the disc jockey took over and the dancing began with the anthem, "Be True To Your School." It was all downwind from there as the Beach Boys, the Beatles, the Outsiders, the Supremes and other shadows of the nostalgic past assumed control of the evening.

Finally, the graduates all knew why they had come back. They had come to renew old ties.

Into the night they danced, shedding the years, the name tags and the inhibitions of adulthood. As the once-quiet kid adjusted the dials, a decade blurred in the flash of lights.

It was a reunion.

Blind, old,
Together
they get by

Mother and daughter have a partnership. Ninety-nine-year-old Zannie tends the garden, and blind Lucinda does the housework.

Perched atop a small bluff on Kansas City's West Side, the two women abide the years together in a little white bungalow. They never venture farther than church, a few miles away.

Neighbors see Zannie Riley daily as she sweeps the porch in back and the sidewalk out front. She dresses in clothing that seems, but isn't, as ancient as she. Shoes and leggings, a housedress and coat, her outfit is topped by a "dust cap" of blue with white polka dots and a narrow frilled brim.

Zannie appears as a vision out of the Old South. In fact, she is a Southerner who came to spend the rest of her days in Kansas City after her husband died. That was in 1951. Zannie never thought she'd have so many days left.

Her only child, Lucinda, took Zannie into the West Side bungalow she shared with her husband, Banks Stevenson, a church deacon and laundryman for the Pullman Co. Stevenson washed sheets and blankets for the railway travelers who criss-crossed the country in Pullman cars.

Lucinda had her sight then, but within a few years an unknown ailment sealed off the visible world.

"The doctors never could find out the trouble," said Lucinda, who is 83 now. "They said I inherited it."

About five years ago Banks Stevenson died and left behind his sightless widow and her mother. The two women were left to fend for themselves. And they have done so.

Lucinda stands behind the stove, stirring greens for lunch. Her hair is braided close to her scalp, and her eyes are hidden by large wire-rimmed sunglasses. She moves without a misstep across the kitchen and into the bathroom, then back into the parlor where photographs preserve images she can only remember.

The floors are clean and the household is neat. The "inside" is Lucinda's territory, where in 25 years of blindness she has learned the place and feel of every object, every surface. She has scrubbed and dusted them.

The "outside" is Zannie's ground. She will be 100 years old December 23, but Zannie Riley still cultivates a patch of peas, okra, tomatoes, beans and collard greens. She has rose bushes and flower boxes to tend.

Her territory begins with the sidewalk out front. Steps lead up to an old porch, framed by ornate wood trim, which wraps around the house and leads to the garden in back. Beyond, an abandoned chicken shack leans precariously next to an alley. The premises, though old, are in order. Zannie Riley makes sure of it.

With assurance she descends the back stairway and looks out over 23rd Street. Her face, brightened by the late summer sun, is a rich brown with lines that arc from prominent cheekbones to the edges of her mouth. Experience has completed Zannie's face and now it has the quality of carved wood.

She laughs to think of her age.

"I am the last and the only one," she says, recalling the mother, father and 12 brothers and sisters whom she has survived. "We was a big family.They are all gone but me. No mother or father, all the sisters and brothers are all gone. I was the baby."

The baby came into this world in Florence, Miss., and worked in the fields through her childhood and into her old age. Her husband, like her father, was a farmer.

"Pick cotton, pull corn," is Zannie's refrain, and she repeats it like a song.

In 1941, daughter Lucinda left the family farm for Kansas City, the big city, where her half sister already was living. Mother and daughter led separate lives in separate places until 1951, when Zannie's husband died and Zannie came to Kansas City.

Now the two rely on each other and the occasional assistance of Gus Moten, a 75-year-old deacon of the Greystone Heights Missionary Baptist Church. Moten was a friend of Banks Stevenson.

"Ever since he died, I come down and help them out," he explains. "I go to the store, or take them someplace, take them to church or help them . . .

"But Sister Riley, she can do more in the garden than I can."

Gus Moten helps. Financial aid from the Social Security Administration helps and so do retirement benefits from the Pullman Co.

Yet the secret of Zannie Riley and Lucinda Stevenson's survival is the secret of a mother and her daughter. One is old and the other is blind — but together they are strong enough.

KC
Society
gets rich
Coverage

Consider the rich, their weddings and cocktail parties, their attention to fashion, their itineraries and obituaries, their alligator shirts and smiles and the marvelous way some of them comb their hair.

Then consider those who consider the rich professionally — the society journalists. In the 1980s the society journalists are working overtime.

Pin it on Ronald Reagan or pin it on hard times if you like; the fact is the well-heeled are suddenly well-liked.

In Kansas City, you can read all about it.

The Independent is the gray lady of society journalism in Kansas City. Staid and 83 years old, it delivers news of the upper crust steadfastly. Every week its columns record the vacation and nuptial doings of old families. Nobody ever dies in the pages of *The Independent,* they simply are referred to in the past tense.

But *The Independent* alone is not adequate for the '80s, it seems. Other publications are muscling in on the moneyed set.

Blvd. is the 3-month-old creation of Hayes Walker III, whose grandfather founded the *American Hereford Journal.* Shifting from cattle to people, Mr. Walker maintains his interest in the well-bred.

However, there's a twist. Mr. Walker does not consider *Blvd.* to be, strictly speaking, a society journal.

Blvd.'s modern look, modeled after the glitzy fashion and society magazine *W,* makes Mr. Walker's monthly magazine a much showier product than *The Independent.*

"I don't think of them (*The Independent*) as competition," avers Mr. Walker, who tried unsuccessfully for two decades to purchase *The Independent.* "They're straight society. We're not straight society. We're running a lot of pictures of people doing things."

By "people doing things" the 48-year-old publisher means Beautiful People attending benefits and parties, wearing the newest fashions and traveling abroad.

In *Blvd.,* Hayes Walker III has whipped up a new journalistic confection — with a dash of Andy Warhol, a dollop of *People* and two cups of *The Independent.*

Rounding out the city's society coverage is *The Kansas City Star* whose new Sunday section, "Star Look," features high fashion and candid pix of KC's not-so-discreet elite at play.

Never, it seems, have so few been so fascinating.

And so sought-after. The formula for society journalism's success is, obviously, that rich people have money. Advertisers want to reach them.

When Mr. Walker says, "I've got great demographics on this book," he means *Blvd.* readers are an advertiser's dream. As Cole Porter once put it, "the tops."

The toniest clothing stores show off their finest merchandise in the pages of society-oriented publications. Travel agencies offer their most expensive travel packages there. Specialty shops and restaurants, too, vie for the glancing eye of the Right People.

But what about the journalism threaded between the ads? Ask Hayes Walker III and he'll tell you his staff concentrates on short stories and pictures, pictures, pictures.

The stories are sometimes spritely, sometimes smarmy, but always upbeat. The magazine's visual style owes equally to the family-album school of photography and modish fashion art.

Never forgotten at *Blvd.* is the publisher's dictum to keep it brief. Referring to another publication in town, Mr. Walker observed, "They're trying to do things in depth — I refuse to do that."

Ask *The Independent,* however, about its thoughts on journalism and it won't tell you anything.

The magazine's publisher since 1939, Mrs. Gleed Gaylord, has declined interviews in recent years. Her staff politely deflects all inquiries.

The Independent, after all, needs no publicity. Like members of the city's most exclusive club, the Kansas City Country Club, the magazine requires no entree because it already has arrived.

The magazine itself abides a long-cherished precept of Kansas City's bluest bloods: simply, that one's name ought not appear in the mass media except in birth, marriage and death.

Birth, marriage and death — with reference to parties, cultural events and vacations in between — provide journalistic fodder for *The Independent,* where the photographs are rooted in the "say-cheese" tradition and the writing is as quiet and languorous as a summer afternoon in Loose Park.

In Kansas City's society journals the living, as ever, is easy.

STREETS
OF THE
CITY

Mailman
delivers
Friendship

You'll see them 'most any morning of the week near Columbus Park.
This morning, it's the corner of Fifth and Harrison. John Lee, the
mailman, is hauling a package to a small sandwich shop. Tagging close
behind him is his sidekick, 14-year-old Charlie Fogle, whose self-
appointed job it is to help John deliver the mail come hell or high
water.

They're an odd couple, these two who walk the streets of Columbus
Park and the nearby Guinotte Manor housing project.

Mailman John is 32 years old, a black man who grew up in a ghetto
to the east. Charlie is a blond-haired, white youth with a broken tooth,
blue eyes and a chip on his shoulder. He's growing up in Guinotte
Manor.

Their friendship began at the close of the school year, when Charlie's
report card arrived via John's mail sack. The mailman could see there
were Fs on the card, and when Charlie came to the door, he wrestled
him playfully and said, "Boy, you do that again and I'm going to
punch you out."

Charlie seemed to like the kindly threat and the next day picked up
with John. The boy didn't have much to do. He couldn't get a job. He
was living with his mother and three younger sisters, getting by on
welfare, fighting a lot with neighborhood kids. Following the mailman
around seemed as good a summer's occupation as any.

At first, Charlie found the route exhausting, but he soon learned to
pace himself. He started "assisting." Recently, he has taken to carrying
a water cup in his back pocket. Whenever he passes a garden hose or
faucet, Charlie fills the cup and hands it to Mailman John.

"Sometimes he's too slow," Charlie protests. "I take off my shoes
and I exercise — push-ups, sit-ups, kickin' up in the air."

Toward the middle of the day, Charlie runs ahead to the dollar
sandwich shop to pick up something for the two of them. They share
lunch. And they talk "man to man."

John and Charlie have a lot to talk about. A 14-year-old boy living
on welfare has a lot of questions. He's also reached a lot of premature
conclusions. Race and money are constantly on Charlie's mind.

In Charlie's housing project neighborhood, there is a variety of ethnic
groups. In his mind, one is pitted against the other. Charlie resents the

Vietnamese particularly because he is convinced they receive more help from the state than the whites, the blacks and the browns.

"They got cars. They got clothes," says Charlie, a little unclearly because he has a mild speech impediment. "A couple of years ago, I didn't have no shoes. I had to walk the hot pavement in my bare feet. So I knocked a kid out and took his shoes."

As Charlie walks around the project, he sees stagnation. There is the stagnation of summer, the idle sounds of children playing in the streets and the youths working on their cars. And there is the stagnation of a slow economy, the sight of able-bodied people without jobs and the constant talk about money, the lack of it. Small children, lying in the street in their underwear, talk about money.

Charlie has found a dependable way to size people up in his neighborhood. He watches their trash and estimates their wealth by what they throw away.

There are many things the mailman's sidekick wants to escape: school, because he is doing "terrible"; other kids who tease him; the poverty of the housing project. Charlie's goal is to become a gardener after he graduates from high school.

"If I can," he says, "I'd like to be outside with plants and flowers and trees." Charlie is growing a bean plant this summer.

John Lee, the mailman, says Charlie is like a lot of the kids he's gotten to know in the neighborhood. He is "perceptive" and "honest" but seems to take his prejudices from elders, says John.

"I don't try to talk down to him," the mailman says. "He talks straight with me. We discuss everything. We talk about racial issues a lot. We discuss all the name-calling."

The mailman tries to set Charlie straight. But the best he can do, he figures, is to take some time with the boy, maybe throw a ball with him. That's what he likes about his job. Being a mailman gives him the opportunity to know people.

He knows them by what they say and how they look. He knows them by the welfare checks they receive, the Social Security checks, the correspondence from relatives and the looks of anticipation when a special letter is expected. He knows them by their mail.

"I'm not regimented," says John, a mailman for 11 years. "I'm not feeling like I'm a cog in some industry. I feel like I'm a vital link with the community between the people here and their grandmother in Nebraska or their girlfriend in Oklahoma."

The mailman is also his sidekick's link to a world outside the housing project.

Call it the
Human Jungle

Barcelona-brand port bottles lie end to end on the window ledge and Rocky Houska sits in the doorway rocking back and forth nervously the way he does, puffing on a hand-rolled cigarette.

He's the one who set the bottles up like that, nice and neat. He did that to improve the area, on Missouri just south of the market square.

Rocky, who's 67, has lived in and around the street since January 20, 1948, when he rode into town on a freight train from South Dakota. He's good with names and dates.

He recalls, for example, that it was Edwin Terry Brigham who ran the Helping Hand Institute, 523 Grand, at that time. On Rocky's first night here, there were 200 other men in the building because they needed a place to stay.

The Helping Hand of Goodwill, as the 85-year-old institution came to be known, closed earlier this month because the number of homeless men here has declined. That's the point of this story.

But Rocky isn't going to miss the place that much. He has learned to survive by not depending on any one thing. You can tell that by looking at him.

Rocky is of medium height, thin, and is wearing a light blue shirt, tawny-colored trousers and black shoes. His silver-white hair is slicked back over the top of his head where he's balding a little. Rocky has a beard but it's not clear whether he made a point of growing it.

About 3 p.m. Tuesday he left the doorway and headed for Sammy's Produce Buffet, a bar, where he talked for a while about the Helping Hand of Goodwill and some of his experiences in Kansas City.

Outside the bar men like Rocky congregated along the sidewalk. Inside the bar, crawfish was the special of the day. Some men were playing pool, others were just drinking.

Rocky, who got his name because he rocks back and forth a lot, explained that currently he is sleeping out under an overhang that keeps the rain off his head. Every morning about 2 or 3 a.m. he goes down to the market and helps unload produce from trucks. It's a steady thing.

He figures there are about a dozen men like himself who stay in the area and sleep out. The others move on to another city or are staying in the transient hotels and shelters for destitute men.

He's a cautious man, he says, a "precautionary man," and that's how he has stayed alive. He remembers one time going into a public bathroom at the market and finding a man stabbed and bleeding.

Rocky has seen plenty of changes since his arrival in 1948. There were a lot of hobos, some bums and not so many winos then, he says. He remembers that the Helping Hand, when Brigham was boss, didn't allow any bottles inside.

But the hobos dwindled in number and those who remained were for the most part alcoholics. Rocky said that made a big difference at the Helping Hand.

"There was all this combustion going on," he related. "All the drinking going on, bringin' bottles in there. You might as well call it the human jungle."

He liked the sound of that. "That's what it is, the human jungle."

Rocky, in his 31 years here, found a lot of other places to stay besides the Helping Hand. The Christian missions, the Salvation Army, Sober House, jail, the outdoors — there was always someplace. Rocky found jobs washing dishes, short-order cooking, unloading.

He remembers sitting in his room a lot of mornings at the Helping Hand, Room No. 80 on the third floor, as the truckers passed by the corner of Missouri and Grand looking for men who needed spot jobs unloading.

The Helping Hand was a focal point for the spot labor market, he says. It was also the place where the "fat market cop" as recently as two weeks ago brought destitute men and dropped them off.

Now that the Helping Hand is closed, Rocky isn't sure what will happen as far as the spot jobs and drunken men go.

Although Rocky has made Kansas City home for all these years, he did leave town once, which he recollects in detail.

"I heard there were some good jobs in Denver so I hopped the Rock Island line on August 10, 1962, and headed west. After we hit Topeka I remember watching the stars and was orienting by them. I realized that we were going in a southwesterly direction. Pretty soon we're in Oklahoma, and eventually we came to Fort Worth."

In Fort Worth, Rocky slept out for the better part of a year but finally landed a job washing dishes at the Gushers Cafe, owned by Bill Daniel. After three weeks, he ran into some trouble at the hands of three young drifters.

"They put the bum on me to buy them a bottle but I didn't have any money. They jumped me and hit me over the shoulder with the empty bottle in the yellow sack they had. Broke my shoulder."

So he hopped a Santa Fe boxcar and returned to Kansas City, June 14, 1963. Been here ever since.

Friends, fares

fill his days

Ray Arzberger is sitting in the driver's seat of his '79 Chevy, a hefty man with twisted legs and a genial personality. Ray looks out through the windshield with glowing blue eyes that look like they're switched onto "hi-beam." He's waiting for a fare.

Not a soul passes by that doesn't say, "Hello." Ray knows 'em all down at the stockyards. Ray just says "how do" and shakes hands. He's waiting for a fare.

Ray looks comfortable in the driver's seat. And well he should. The driver's seat has been home to Ray Arzberger most of his 69 years. Crippled by polio when he was just 5 months old, Ray drives for a living. For more than 30 years he's been waiting for fares and driving as a private cabbie and mobile night watchman down in the stockyards district.

The waitresses who work in the restaurants and bars down there pick up rides from Ray. So do workers in the Livestock Exchange Building. And the livestock handlers as well.

"How do," says Ray. And they're off, supported by the gypsy cabman's flawless driving record and his CB radio.

Ray's a good talker, as many cabbies are. And he knows how to keep a story short, especially if you're getting off at the next block. The highlights of Ray's life make for an entertaining ride.

He can tell you about the days when he used to drive William Allen White around. Ray grew up in Emporia, Kansas, the home of the famous Kansas newspaper editor and publisher, and when Ray was in elementary school his mother worked as a housekeeper for White.

"In those days," says Ray, "you didn't need a driver's license. They never heard of insurance. As long as you could see over the steering wheel you could drive."

So the schoolboy with the crippled legs ran errands for White in a Model T Ford touring car. Whenever White was going out of town, his butler would load up the Model T, and Ray would transport the luggage to the Santa Fe rail depot.

"William Allen White was a great man," says Ray. "He had a butler, a chauffeur, a limousine and a housekeeper."

When Ray was 14 years old, he remembers, "I went to work for a fellow named Jeff Wheat, a little humpbacked man. He was a horse

24

and mule buyer. We'd go out to the farms in my Model T and buy horses and mules. Whenever he wanted to buy, he'd lay that cane of his on his arm. If he didn't want to buy, he'd just use it to walk away with."

Times were rough in the 1930s and Ray, who couldn't find work, decided he'd leave Kansas to seek his fortune. Roving through Oklahoma in a 1929 Model A Ford sedan, he looked all around but never did find a job. In 1936, Ray drifted to Kansas City and signed on as a truck driver.

Ray lived in the Victor Hotel at 1507 Genessee and drove for trucking concerns in the stockyards district. Those were the good old days there. Ray remembers five hotels on the block and he can rattle off the names of the saloons: the Buckhorn, the Cowboy Inn, the Silver Dollar Saloon and the Wyoming Club.

It was years before the insurance companies caught on to Ray Arzberger, the trucker with the bum legs. Eventually, they forced him out of the truck. They said he was a hazard, although he says he has never had an accident.

After that, Ray started his cab business. The stockyards district was a little rough around the edges and many regular cabbies stayed away from the area. Ray picked up the slack. He ran into some trouble of his own.

"Oh, I've had a lot of trouble in my time," he says. "I can be pretty tough . . ."

There was the time outside the Wyoming Club when "five ruffians from Armourdale" interfered while Ray was trying to push a musician friend's car out of a snow bank.

"They opened the car door on the passenger side and one of 'em crawled in and I beat the soup out of him," Ray remembers. "The others tried the same thing. I whipped all five of 'em before it was over."

That story may have improved with time. Ray says his driving career has improved as well. In addition to giving rides, he works as a watchman for several companies in the area. Ray patrols the district and if he sees anything suspicious he notifies the police.

"I made a living here 43 years — a good living," he says. "Everybody's my friend. I don't got money, but I don't need money. I figure a million friends — a dollar apiece — and I'm a millionaire."

It's been years since the Victor Hotel closed and Ray had to seek lodging elsewhere. It's been years since the stockyards district buzzed with activity, too. But Ray's still driving around down there.

He
Can't
go home
Anymore

It had been Jimmy's fate to spend his days and nights cleaning up the
12th Street Strip.

To many the Strip was the last vestige of a heyday gone sour — seedy
bars, rundown hotels, a peep show. But to Jimmy Harris it was home.
To many the Strip was a decaying example of tawdry, commercialized
sex. But to Jimmy it was a living.

To those who drive or walk by the row of buildings between
Wyandotte and Central the Strip must have seemed a haven for outcasts
and hustlers. To Jimmy the people there were family.

It was last May that Jimmy arrived in Kansas City and just naturally
gravitated toward 12th Street.

Young, tough-looking, retarded — Jimmy Harris had a few strikes
against him. At first sight, he looked dangerous. With straight black
hair and sharply angled features, with blue eyes that highlight a fair
complexion, with 32 years behind him and nearly half of them in
psychiatric or custodial care, Jimmy hit the street like a ton of bricks.

He just naturally gravitated to 12th Street.

At first, he worked for room and board at a downtown hotel, but
soon he reached an agreement with the operators of Bonnie & Clyde's
Lounge. He would help out by making sure supplies were in stock; he
would run errands and pick up takeout orders; he would take out the
trash.

Jimmy worked cheap. Pretty soon, he said, he was working for most
of the joints along the Strip: the It Club, Pal Joey's, the Other Room,
the Two Twenty Two, the Park Plaza. He moved to the Hill Hotel,
right on the Strip.

"I'd walk from place to place, in and out, from 10 in the morning
till closing time," Jimmy said. "I liked it. You'd never know from one
day to the next what it would be. I liked to keep the places clean, keep
those trash bags moving. I always made sure there was plenty of beer in
the case, and plenty of ice."

After a while, Jimmy became a fixture on 12th Street. He'd be seen a lot at the Pioneer Grill on Baltimore picking up orders. He came to know the bartenders, the dancers, the owners, the cop on the beat. Working on and off at a flower shop on Baltimore, he'd have flowers to give to the hookers who drove by in their cars. The dancers got flowers as well.

Jimmy took his pay in a different way. He didn't earn money by the hour or the day. Instead, he kept the change a lot. His employers gave him tickets to see the Chiefs, the Kings, the Royals. People frequently "loaned" him money. He scraped what he could from the top. And he rolled with it.

"It's a job," he explained. "That's the most important thing."

By the end of the year, Jimmy had been out of the hospital more than eight months straight, his longest absence in 15 years.

It could have been said that some of the people on the Strip were taking advantage of him. But there could be no denying that, for Jimmy, getting by on the street was a lot better than getting by in some hospital ward.

Only 9 years old when he was first determined to be retarded, Jimmy ended up at the Osawatomie State Hospital in 1968. He has harsh words for life at a state hospital: "They keep people drugged up. They don't talk to people like they should. They lock 'em up and leave 'em alone. Some of them commit suicide."

A "graduate" of Osawatomie, Jimmy still has problems, he will admit. He said he finds it difficult to live around so much crime. Sometimes he tells people off. He's been hit, but Jimmy said he isn't afraid of the knives and guns the pimps carry.

Some of his friends, however, do fear for him. Linda Gray is one. Thirty years old and working as a bartender at a downtown lounge, Linda was a dancer on the Strip for eight years. When the city told the inhabitants of the block to make way for the proposed hotel, Linda tried to find Jimmy another place to work and live. "He calls me 'Sis,'" she explained.

Brenda Humphries is another friend. She works behind the bar at Judy Ann's, which is run by the former operators of the It Club, in the East Bottoms. Brenda said: "The bartenders, the girls and the owners have kind of looked out for him . . . Sometimes he's like a little boy. He calls me 'Mom.'"

Now Jimmy lives above Judy Ann's and works there in the mornings. Since all the businesses were closed down on the Strip, he has managed to find work at various places around town, some of them owned by his former employers. He has a regular daily route, traveling by bus from establishment to establishment.

The Strip is virtually gone. The buildings are still there, but the banter of the pimps and the sounds of the jukebox have moved on. So has Jimmy Harris, who once knew the place as home and got his start there.

For Ben, Freedom's a Must

It's a familiar sight. The light turns red on the corner of 12th and Washington. He jumps the curb in his wheelchair and wheels out into traffic while the cars are stopped.

"Hey, buddy, got a quarter?"

The answer may be yes; the answer may be no. Either way, it's OK with Ben Arnold. He figures he'll get by.

Arnold, 55, is one of the downtown area's best known figures. In the concrete garden he is a perennial.

He's hard to miss. Ben's lost both his legs and relies on strong arms and a wheelchair for locomotion. A blue knit cap covers his gray hair. His beard is full and almost white. His skin is leathery and deeply tanned. Ben is a kind of "sailor of the streets."

Ben has divided his time during the last three years between the streets of downtown and the Municipal Correctional Institution, where he frequently serves short sentences for minor offenses.

For men like Ben, the municipal facility is sometimes a haven. Ben leads an unpredictable life. The whims of the elements and the street can be unforgiving. A 30-day sentence means 30 days of shelter and meals.

But while Ben admits that sometimes he needs to be arrested — "been drinkin' too much or something" — he prefers his freedom.

"I like to be free. I like the streets," he says with a smile. "In the warm weather I sleep out. I just have a quilt on top. I sleep in old buildings or some people put me up."

When it's colder, Ben is sometimes known to spend nights over the heating vent next to the Barickman Advertising building at 12th and Washington. He says he's pretty well-known to the employees there, but hastens to add that he's been arrested for trespassing on occasion.

Ben's "territory" stretches from Main on the east to Jefferson on the west, and from 9th Street to 17th, he says.

Within those boundaries he has found people willing to help him in a variety of ways. The cops who give him an even break or make sure he's doing all right on a cold night; the liquor store operator who keeps Ben's unused artificial legs in his basement; the merchants who provide for some of his needs — they are a network of people who care about Ben.

"Anywhere I go downtown, people holler to me. They give me money or something to eat. They say, 'How you doin', Ben? You need a quarter?' One time a guy gave me a bill and I was talkin' to him. I didn't see 'til after he left that it was a 20.

"Every once in a while, you get somebody who says, 'Why don't you get a job?' But that don't bother me," he adds.

Ben came to Kansas City three years ago under circumstances best described as tragic.

At the time, he had been working as a drill press operator for an auto manufacturer in Detroit. Until that point in his life, Ben had worked in many cities, had hoboed around the country on freight trains some and was no stranger to Missouri, where his sister lived.

Ben says he hadn't been in a boxcar in 2½ years but just got an itch to ride the rails. "I had plenty of money on me," he recalls. "I just felt like doin' it."

In a train yard in Olathe, Ben hopped out of a car that was moving too fast. Suction from underneath the car pulled him under the wheels, and his legs were severed. Ben believes he would have bled to death right there if the switchmen hadn't come to his aid quickly. At the hospital he required 12½ pints of blood, he says.

Since then, Ben has lived off the streets, with occasional financial help from a sister in Arizona. His survival downtown testifies to his resourcefulness, and it says something about Ben's strongest need: to be free.

"I don't like those nursing homes," he says. "I've been in one twice and I don't like 'em. It'd be different if I couldn't get around. I know I look old, but I don't like to be cooped up."

Of course, freedom has its limits. As officials at the Municipal Correctional Institution are quick to point out, Ben's network of friends is most visible during the day. At night, he often is left to fend for himself. So it's not surprising that Ben frequently finds himself back in city custody.

He hit the streets on Wednesday, finishing up a 30-day stint, and says he plans to spend the holidays with a friend on the East Side.

Undoubtedly, Ben Arnold will be seen again working the corner of 12th and Washington, wheeling into traffic to panhandle a quarter, shouting from the sidewalk to the motorists passing by.

Maybe then he'll roll down to 12th and Main, where there's always a lot of pedestrian traffic, and say hello to his acquaintances along that route.

"If I got enemies," says Ben, "I don't know who they are."

Henderson lives in a
Drifter's Hotel...

From his room on the third floor of the Cordova Hotel, 12th and Pennsylvania, Warren Henderson observes a straggling procession of humanity.

They are the transients, mostly men who are headed somewhere else. They stay in hotels like the Cordova and then they move on.

Henderson is the resident "houseman" at the hotel and helps out with miscellaneous chores. If a man hitchhikes in from another town or rides in on the rails, Henderson is there with advice. He sees them come and go. Recently, he saw me come and go . . .

It is 6 p.m. on a Monday night. The wind blows across the bluff downtown and few are on the streets. Only the winos and the johns bother to go out on such a night.

I check into the Cordova Hotel and the deskman asks for six dollars. Then he sends for Shorty, the bellman. Shorty leads me up two flights of stairs past Henderson's room, where the smell of cooking and the sound of a television drift out into the musty hallway.

I can see through the door that Henderson's room has a lived-in quality to it. Several men have joined him for some television. The men are talking.

Shorty leads me to Room 304 on the east side of the building facing the nearby Roslin Hotel. It is a pale blue chamber, about 8×10 feet, with high ceilings. The sink fixtures there have been ripped out, and the exposed pipes are covered by a bed sheet tacked to the wall. The discarded sink lies on its side in the closet. The bathroom is down the hall.

There are no sheets on the bed, so Shorty goes to find Henderson, who returns with Cordova Hotel linen, muttering, "I ain't the maid." The sheet is clean but the letters "CH" have been spray-painted on in red.

Left alone in the room, I sprawl on the bed to ponder my prospects and to rest. Except for the faint sound of Henderson's television, all is quiet.

On a Monday night in downtown Kansas City, there isn't a whole lot to do. A block west on 12th, four drunks are holding court in Club 605, where crudely painted nudes adorn the wall and Christmas decorations hang over the bar.

A few blocks away on Washington, the patrons of Allen's Bar & Restaurant are drinking, finishing dinner and watching "Monday Night Football." Three stony-faced men in the Cordova lobby are watching the game, too.

Growing restive, I fumble through the drawers of the dresser in 304, to see whether the room offers anything more than shelter.

In the top drawer I find evidence of an earlier occupant: an empty cigarette package, an empty pint bottle of Seagram's, a fork, a burnt match and a worn copy of *The Methuselah Enzyme,* a novel by Fred Mustard Stewart about rejuvenation.

The paperback has "Eugene Public Library" stamped across its pages and inside, across the title page, there is a handwritten list. It is a personal inventory of some sort:

1 broken watch, 1 broken pen, 1 bedroll, 2 blankets, 3 shirts, 2 pants, 1 jacket, 2 coffee cups, 1½ gal. water, 1 pr. tennis shoes, 1 Book of Mormon, 1 modern trans. Bible, 1 frying pan, 1 nudie magazine, .06 cash.

The inside pages are crowded with columns of gambling wins and losses. The gambler has also left a brief log: *Left Eugene, Ore. Tues. around noon went to K. Falls then Ogden Utah then N. Platt Neb. (stopped somewhere in Wyo. but I didn't get up and see where).*

Who was the writer? He came from Eugene, but where did he go? Henderson doesn't remember him. The secret seems safe with Room 304.

I drop off to sleep reading *The Methuselah Enzyme.* In the morning I leave, but my departure is not noted particularly. There is no key to return. The faces in the lobby are expressionless as I walk out onto 12th Street.

I might have been just another in the straggling procession of transients who stay for a few days' work or panhandling and then move on to another indifferent town.

Their numbers decline at this time of year, Henderson explains, but they come all the same, those who are "unlucky enough to happen to get stuck here."

Most of the drifters head south about now. Henderson, who is 68 and lost most of his eyesight working in the steel mills of Pittsburgh, says they go to Florida, or Texas, or some other state along the Gulf. Henderson calls them "snowballs" for some reason, these men who follow the sun.

While they're here in Kansas City, Henderson tries to steer them right. It's clear he prefers his own style of life. "As long as I have a roof over my head and three meals, I'm satisfied," he says.

"That wanderin' around, that's not for me."

...and
Dies
one morning,
Leaving
the bill

Warren Henderson was a rolling stone in life and in death. He didn't gather much moss.

When he died last week at the Labor Pool, his friends and local authorities looked hard for some kin to pay for Warren's burial. But they were unsuccessful and now his embalmed body lies on a slab in the University of Missouri-Kansas City School of Dentistry morgue, awaiting the scalpel of a student ready to learn anatomy.

It is perhaps an unceremonious way to go out, piece by piece under the glare of laboratory lights. But that's what can happen to people who have lost track of their families, who carry nothing in their wallets but slips of paper with defunct telephone numbers on them.

Henderson was like that. He was like a lot of the men who live in the downtown area's transient hotels. Henderson had worked for a steel mill in Pittsburgh, but the job cost him some of his eyesight. He moved to Kansas City and worked more casually through the Labor Pool, an agency that places men in temporary jobs.

Henderson had a room for a time at the Cordova Hotel on West 12th Street. It was a decent room, and he improved it with a stereo and television. Henderson was employed as the "houseman" at the hotel, and many of the men there got to know him well. Henderson's room was a poor man's social parlor.

The night before he died, Warren dropped by the old place (for by this time he had moved to the New Fredric Hotel on East Ninth Street) and bought his pal Brownie a beer. It seems curious now that he paid for the round, when back at the New Fredric he owed two weeks' back rent. Warren Henderson was not known for getting behind in his rent.

He wasn't like some of the fellows he got to know downtown. A lot of them were drifters, arriving by rail or bus or thumb to work for a few days or perhaps to panhandle and then move on. Henderson helped some of these men out, but he made a point of saying, "As long as I have a roof over my head and three meals, I'm satisfied. That wanderin' around, that's not for me."

Warren used to talk quite a bit about a daughter of his who lived in Kansas City. This was a curious thing, because later on no one could find her.

October 23 started like many days for Henderson. He arrived at the Labor Pool, 1910 Main, about 6:30 a.m. and sat down to wait for work.

But since nobody seemed to need his labor that Thursday, Henderson dozed off in his chair, as he was known to do. Nobody thought much of it until he made an odd sound and fell off the chair. Heart attack. An ambulance was called. The paramedics tried to revive him, but by the time Warren Henderson got to the emergency room, his life was over.

Through the rest of that day and most of the next, the Jackson County medical examiner's office and some of his friends tried to locate Warren's relations. He had told Leroy Tryan, a pal at the Cordova Hotel, that he had a daughter named Hazel Hartman who was a nurse at St. Luke's Hospital and was married to a doctor. If anything should ever happen to him, Henderson told Leroy, Leroy was to call Hazel. He did. But the hospital had never heard of her.

An employee in the medical examiner's office, Carmen Rhodelander, managed to locate Henderson's brother in Philadelphia. The brother gave Ms. Rhodelander the names of Warren's children, who were supposed to be living in other cities. But none of the names checked out. Ms. Rhodelander called the brother back and said the children couldn't be found. The brother said he hadn't seen Warren for five years and there was nothing he could do for him. The brother hung up.

There was no one to pay for Henderson's burial — he had only 85 cents on him when he died; no next of kin could be found to pay; the Veterans Administration had no record of Warren's service career, so it would not pay.

If Henderson's body had been unsatisfactory for the purposes of science, the county would have paid $255 for a pauper's burial. But Henderson was in pretty good shape, and the county was spared the expenditure.

The body was sent to the Morticians Embalming Service, 538 Campbell, and then shipped to the dental school. The school will hold the body for 30 days before using it, just in case Warren's family is found.

After that, the body of Warren Henderson will leave behind a world of lost connections, broken families and drifters passing in the night. He will go to science.

Back at the New Fredric Hotel, the desk clerk is keeping Henderson's property in the storage room. There is the matter of two weeks' rent.

KANSAS CITY
HERE I COME

What's
in a name?
Lots in old
KC

Back in the good old days, "Possum Trot" was briefly considered as a name for the city now known as Kansas City. Since the annual Possum Trot celebration is being held this weekend at the stockyards, it seems a good time to review the facts and controversies surrounding the selection of a name for our humble burg on the river.

Even the briefest of reviews, however, cannot fail to note that, although things might be on the "up and up" today, back in 1838, KC's founding fathers marched into history through the muck of a riot, a bamboozlement and what likely was a rather boozy naming ceremony.

Details of the riot, a seminal event in Kansas City history, remain somewhat obscure. This much is known: in November of 1831, a brawl broke out in the French community encamped near the mouth of the Kansas River. Lying dead amid the blood and mud was one Gabriel Prudhomme, who left behind a pregnant wife and six children.

The county court appointed guardians for Prudhomme's heirs, and seven years later, at the request of the family, the court ordered a public sale of the Prudhomme farm, which consisted of more than 250 acres on the south shore of the Missouri River.

The sale, however, was marred by charges of bamboozlement when it turned out that the auctioneer, James Hyatt McGee, had reached a prior agreement with Abraham Fonda, the self-described "gentleman" who offered the winning bid of $1,800. McGee was one of the "guardians" of the heirs, to boot.

A second sale was held in November of 1838, and this time $4,220 bought the farm for a town company composed of prominent locals organized hastily by Capt. William L. Sublette, the famous mountain man. Also in the town company was Abraham Fonda (who had a strong hankering for that land) and the famous John C. McCoy.

McCoy had already established a store in Westport for the purpose of trading with the Indians to the west. He had discovered that the Prudhomme farm, which included a natural landing at the river, also was a promising site for a future settlement.

Sometime after the sale, the 14 members of the town company retired to discuss the future in the home of a dubious character by the name of One-Eyed Ellis. In the brief meeting that ensued, Ellis found his place in history, although none has ever burdened his reputation with greatness.

He was best known as a denizen of the bluff area who sold bad whiskey to the Indians.

Since One-Eyed was often in the vicinity of the landing, he was frequently called upon to witness commercial transactions, as required by law. On the basis of this experience, Ellis was named chairman of the town company naming ceremony. He deftly drew out a blue-backed Webster's spelling book for the occasion and started looking up some words.

No good words were found for a name, however, and in the discussion that followed, Abraham Fonda argued that the town ought to be called Port Fonda. Why he chose this name is unknown.

Fonda apparently was shouted down, however, and other suggestions were made. One man suggested Rabbitville, but this too failed to win over the assemblage. Then Possum Trot was proffered, and again, for reasons unknown, the town remained nameless. Finally, with rabbits, possums and Fonda ruled out, the town company reached its momentous decision.

It would be the Town of Kansas, after the nearby river and Indian tribe. History made, One-Eyed Ellis gaveled the meeting to a close and slipped back into obscurity below the bluff.

The town grew very slowly at first, and in fact the founding fathers had to be hauled into court to pay off their original debt to the Prudhomme family. John C. McCoy was unenthusiastic about the town, its name and its future, and dismissed the idea that it would amount to something as the "idle vaporings of a demented intellect."

Incorporated as a city in 1853, Kansas City did amount to something, surprising as that may be.

But the naming ceremony at Ellis' shack has haunted our fair town. If, for example, old One-Eyed had come up with something in that blue-backed Webster's, perhaps we'd have a different name, one that didn't cause so much confusion.

Unfortunately, "Kansas City" has been an endless source of confusion.

The fact that Kansas City is in Missouri has eluded some of the greatest minds of our times. The land to the west was named the Kansas Territory some years after the meeting at the shack. And consequently, the state of Kansas stole old One-Eyed's thunder.

We need an honest
Boss
Tom

Say Tom Pendergast's name, and most Kansas Citians will gasp. Boss Tom is still taboo in this town, more than 40 years after his political demise.

And yet there is a lingering body of opinion that holds that Pendergast, for all his faults, was a can-do politician whose minions made the 1920s and 1930s the most dynamic and upward-bound period in the city's history.

There are those who look at the do-nothing lethargy of the present and say, "Tom Pendergast, where are you now that we need you?"

Kansas City attorney Arthur A. Benson II, while no booster of Pendergast, agrees that the city of today could use some of the ambition and drive of yesterday. To bring it back, he has proposed a city charter change that would strengthen the mayor's office. A stronger mayor, he reasons, could ignite new drive in a city that clearly has lost its vigor.

There are those who see the ghost of Pendergast in the proposal. And there are those who welcome it, like the man who wrote to Mr. Benson, "At least Pendergast and McElroy (Henry McElroy, the city manager) knew how to get things done."

All the ghosts and paranoia aside, is there anything to the contention that the strong figure of Pendergast brought eminence to this town?

Yes. Even Pendergast's formidable detractors, *Kansas City Star* editors Henry C. Haskell Jr. and Richard B. Fowler, conceded that point.

"Here were men," they wrote of Pendergast and his lieutenants, "in some respects nearer the mold of Kansas City's great civic leaders than its usual political leaders. They were builders, men of action and dreamers of monumental things. They had caught something of that native Kansas City spirit from the generation of William Rockhill Nelson and August Meyer."

Back then, when these builders and dreamers were at the helm, Kansas City was in an expansive mood, and a great many edifices were erected: the Fidelity National Bank building, the Bryant building, the skyscraping Power & Light Building and the Nelson Art Gallery, to name a few.

Operating in the public domain, these politicians persuaded voters to back the famous Ten Year Plan, an enormous program financed by $40 million in bonds and passed in 1931, in the depths of the Depression, by a margin of 4-1.

(Recall that only recently the mayor of Kansas City was incapable of persuading voters to support a half-cent sales tax to make long-neglected repairs in Kansas City's infrastructure of roads, sidewalks and bridges.)

In succeeding years Kansas City embarked on an unprecedented campaign that would see the erection of Municipal Auditorium, City Hall, the Music Hall, the Jackson County Courthouse and Police Headquarters.

A baseball stadium was built to house the triple-A Kansas City Blues, and a fortune was spent paving Brush Creek, at that time described as a repugnant little stream carrying sewage to the Blue River.

Of course, Boss Pendergast's Ready-Mixed Concrete company benefited nicely from that project. But so did the ordinary laborers of the city. They found jobs when the rest of the country was out of work.

Indeed there are those who contend it was Kansas City that developed the working model for Franklin Roosevelt's New Deal public works projects. It was Henry McElroy, the city manager, who first created a successful program to put Kansas City's unemployed to work during the first winter of the Depression.

Labor-saving equipment was put aside whenever possible, according to historian Lyle Dorsett, and more than 20,000 people were employed in Mr. McElroy's projects.

In July 1933, FDR's right-hand man, Harry Hopkins, sent his assistants to Kansas City to study the operation. Soon after, the Roosevelt administration unveiled its Civil Works Administration program of work relief projects.

The New deal was an especially good deal for Kansas City because Pendergast's influence in federal and state government brought the preponderance of federal jobs to the city. As historians Dorsett and A. Theodore Brown have noted, "A major share of the 110,000 men and women employed in Missouri by CWA were in the Kansas City metropolitan area."

Back in those days, Kansas City was truly a hub, the 19th-largest city in the nation (as compared to its current ranking of 27th) and the biggest town between St. Louis and Los Angeles. A rail town then, we are an air town now, but as anybody who has visited Kansas City International airport lately will tell you, we are not quite the capital we once were. On some days, it seems that nobody leaves or arrives in Kansas City at all.

The verdict on Tom Pendergast? Sure, he was a corrupt politician and deserved to go to jail. But he was a strong figure who accomplished much. We sorely need another.

New York kid
Creates
a KC
Classic

Bruce Ricker was just another overheated New Yorker, "stranded" in Kansas City and searching desperately for action, hovering in dimly lit places only to lurch into the limelight briefly when there was action to be had.

He talked fast, had dark curly hair and a perpetual 5 o'clock shadow. He hustled leftist political issues, literature, exploitation movies and counterculture heroes. In short, he was everything many conservative Midwesterners instinctively distrust.

And so it is either ironic or fitting — I can't figure out which — that it was Bruce Ricker who made "The Last of the Blue Devils," a film that captures the essence of Kansas City's native art form, jazz. The film opens Friday at area theatres.

Jazz has been in Kansas City's back yard since the '20s, but it took a character from Staten Island to tell the world about it. A part of the story from the singing bartender, Big Joe Turner:

Well, I been to Kansas City
Oh, everything is really alright

Ricker came to Kansas City in 1970 to teach law school and earn an advanced degree in urban studies. He styled himself "counselor" to many literary magazines and underground publications, acting as a writer at times and at other times as legal counsel.

Ricker and a band of protesters stormed the *Kansas City Times* in the wake of Richard Nixon's decision to mine North Vietnam's harbors. The protesters marched into the news room, and David Perkins, now editor of the literary magazine *Chouteau Review,* leaped atop an editor's desk to demand access to the newspaper's columns.

Yes, I been to Kansas City
Well, and everything is really alright

Ricker began to make some inroads into the established political community, somehow landing a job as assistant city prosecutor in charge of juvenile cases.

"We were all interested in power and bucks," remembers David Perkins, speaking for the political underground of that time. "The guys who had the power were interested in dope and wild women."

That may or may not be true, but when the underground met the mainstream in KC, the sparks began to fly. The lid blew off in 1973 when Ricker threw a party at his house. There were the usual loud music and marijuana. A county legislator was there and, sensing certain contradictions in the air, he succeeded in having Ricker fired from his job as prosecutor.

And the boys'll jump and swing
Well, until broad daylight

"Bruce was always stirring up something, trying to be part of it, trying to make something happen," remembers one friend. Eventually, he started stirring up some movies.

One of the first he helped make was "Linda Lovelace for President," a relatively benign follow-up to Ms. Lovelace's notorious "Deep Throat." The makers of "Linda Lovelace for President" managed to touch off a controversy at the University of Kansas when they persuaded administrators to let members of the KU basketball team appear in the film carrying a "Linda Lovelace for President" banner at the head of a parade. The marching band provided the soundtrack.

Yes, I dreamed last night
I was standing on 18th und Vine

A lover of rock 'n' roll and jazz from his days as an "alienated adolescent," Ricker naturally gravitated to the Mutual Musicians Foundation at 18th & Highland, where he listened to the all-night jazz jams held there. There he developed a friendship with Ernie Williams, the aging drummer of the Blue Devils band. Williams spoke even faster than Ricker.

Sensing that a long-overdue jazz film could be made, Ricker brought the old jazzmen together in 1974. Among the many were Count Basie, Jay McShann, Big Joe Turner and Jesse Price. Price arrived in Kansas City a very sick man and sang for posterity, "You can't take it with you over to the Promised Land."

Three days later he died, after sending a thank-you telegram to Ricker.

Yes I dreamed last night
I was standing on 18th and Vine

For Ricker the film was a labor of love, a piece of action with lasting value. After making it he returned to New York and spent three years raising enough money to complete the editing. In that time another of the film's characters, Richard Smith, died.

The era recedes into history. But the film ensures that its heroes will survive.

Well I shook hands with Piney Brown
Well I just couldn't keep from crying.

Greek's
chicken begot
Bird

Had he lived, Charlie Parker would have been 61 years old today, a musician of distinguished vintage. But this column does not concern Charlie Parker, the 61-year-old who never was. Rather, it is about the days when "Bird" Parker was an impetuous youth who got his nickname from the streetside delicacies of a Kansas City Greek called John Agnos.

Like Parker's music, Agnos' legacy lives. If you don't believe that, go down to 12th & Forest sometime and see the modern-day version of John Agnos' Famous Sandwiches store.

The takeout-sandwich shop, now run by Agnos' nephew, still sells pig snoot sandwiches and more. But the surroundings have changed. The 12th Street strip of yesteryear is gone. Agnos' shop is surrounded by vacant lots and half-demolished buildings instead of the saloons, shops and residences that once were.

Back then, when the legendary era was in full sway, a fellow named Charlie came to be called "Bird." There are different explanations for how Parker got the name, which was shortened from "Yardbird." One of the more durable legends goes this way:

In the '30s, while still too young to enter a nightclub, Parker used to hang around the back lot of the famous Reno Club, where he idolized the mature jazzmen like Lester Young and Count Basie who played inside. As jazz historian Ross Russell tells it in *Bird Lives!*, drummer Jesse Price befriended the youthful saxophonist and helped him gain surreptitious entry to the club so he could listen to the music. Price and others got to calling Charlie "Yardbird," the colloquial word for chicken, because Parker ate so many of the "short thighs" sold by Agnos in the back lot of the club.

John Agnos is dead now, and so is Parker. But Agnos' nephew, of the same name, resides on West 88th Street and remembers the history and nature of his rough-and-ready uncle.

"My uncle was a sharp guy who drove a big Buick touring car," said Agnos.

One of a wave of Greek immigrants coming to Kansas City around the turn of the century, Agnos started his sandwich business in 1909 on a chicken wing and a prayer. Agnos sold strictly American food from a horsedrawn buckboard, which he had painted white with red trim.

According to Agnos' nephew, Agnos offered his customers a menu that included pork tenderloins, chicken, fish, pig snoots, pig ears, pigs' feet, hot dogs, brain sandwiches and even Limburger cheese.

Agnos expanded and modernized with time. Instead of a single wagon being hauled down 15th Street, he had four, and a fifth was at 12th and Forest. Operating from 4 p.m. to 4 a.m., to serve the day crowd and the night revelers as well, Agnos left his lanterns at home and hooked up gas and electric lines to nearby shops.

Agnos became very successful, partly because he was a good business-man and partly because political boss Tom Pendergast granted him a monopoly in the area.

In the meantime, Agnos' brother Simeon operated his own restaurants and Simeon's son John began to learn about chicken and brain sandwiches and pig snoots.

The 1940s, however, brought changes to Kansas City that eventually would be the kiss of death to Agnos' horse-drawn wagons:

Pendergast went to jail. Many of the jazz musicians, including Bird Parker, went to other cities. War made a Marine aviator out of John Agnos' nephew.

In 1946, City Hall outlawed Agnos' wagons because they didn't have running water. The wagons were junked, leaving only a small restaurant at 12th & Forest, which Agnos operated until 1961, when his nephew bought the business.

The elder John Agnos has been dead about five years now, and his sandwich shop is being run by the younger John Agnos, his wife, Paula, and their youngest son, Jim. They don't stay open weekends or late into the night anymore (just 9:30 a.m. to 3:30 p.m.); they take vacations (they're on one now and won't be back until Monday); and they've witnessed 12th Street's profound transformation from a lively street life district to the home of light industry and warehouses.

Yet still, people drive up to the takeout window at 12th & Forest and talk to Agnos about his Uncle John. They talk about the jazz, the "great turnover of human beings," as Agnos puts it, and they still eat those famous sandwiches.

If he were alive today, there's little doubt about what Bird Parker would be eating.

The state of the
City
is a
Puzzle

A trip east is usually interesting, if only because a Kansas Citian learns what the Easterners are thinking or (as is more usually the case) what they are not thinking about Kansas City.

What they most often are not thinking about Kansas City is that it is in Missouri.

"How's Kansas?" they say.

At first, you answer somewhat pedantically that Kansas City is in Missouri.

"That's Kansas City, *Missouri*," you say.

They look at you like you're from Newfoundland. They really want to say, "So who cares? Kansas, Missouri, Oklahoma — what do people do out there?" But they don't bother to say it. They're so busy.

My recent trip into this morass began, as usual, with the drive to Kansas City International Airport, which is a remarkably convenient airport since hardly anybody else is there taking up space in ticket counter lines and parking lots.

It occurred to me — as I was swiftly ushered from the parking lot, through the non-existent ticket line and onto the airplane — that one reason nobody knows KC is in Missouri is that so few of us seem to be going anywhere to represent the city on this matter.

If more people went to the airport and on to the big cities of the world, why then, there might be a Kansas Citian on every street corner advising the world's citizens that it's "Kansas City, *Missouri*."

Then the burden wouldn't fall on my shoulders (but, I guess, other Kansas City travelers fancy they are shouldering the burden alone, too).

After being whisked aboard a half-empty eastbound aircraft, I found myself seated next to a young man busily licking stamps and fastening them to business-sized envelopes. There appeared to be at least 50 envelopes stacked in piles on the floor, seat and seat-back table. I imagined that this young Kansas Citian was engaged in some sort of political campaign.

Maybe he worked for the National Conservative Political Action Committee or the World Wildlife Federation and was trying to save conservatives and kill whales or vice versa.

But, no, of course not. He was an Easterner trying his best to find a new job so he could depart Kansas City, Missouri, and return to his beloved coast where all the action was. The letters were all job applications.

"I work for the (well-known product) company, headquartered here and, boy, is it a snooze," he said cheerfully. "I'm looking to get out of here."

Well, I thought, fair enough. To each his own. If he doesn't like it, let him go to New Jersey. Serves him right.

In the interests of boosting Kansas City's image, however, I began to tell this man about all the marvelous restaurants and out-of-the-way haunts he probably hadn't seen yet.

Naturally, he'd seen them all. Yes, all the fried chicken, barbecue, steak, Mexican food and seafood joints that it took you and me years to find — the Easterner had been to every one.

As Trans World Airlines disgorged us into the teeming LaGuardia Airport in New York, I wished him the best. With luck, perhaps he would find that job working for a parts manufacturer in Passaic, I said.

I don't think he could hear me, though, on account of the booming hordes of New York travelers who swallowed us up in the crowded concourse. None of them, I was sure, was going to Kansas City and, even if they were, they wouldn't know what state they were going to.

The weekend passed in a blur of fireworks and smiling faces asking, "So, tell me, what's it like in Kansas?"

It has to be admitted that only the most faithful Kansas Citian can stand up long under such duress. The feigned politeness, the patient explanation, "Uh, that's Kansas City, *Missouri*" — these key elements of the booster's educational program slowly are replaced with a grimace and the phrase, "Very nice, thank you."

My weekend trip wound down with a return to LaGuardia Airport and the usual struggle to hack my way through the crowds to the desolate terminal where a few Kansas Citians were awaiting takeoff for home.

On board the half-empty plane, I listened in as a brand-new Kansas Citian shouted in a Brooklyn accent to another passenger, "Yeah, I just got transferred. I'm lookin' for a house. It's just me and the wife. Hey, how many people live in Kansas City, anyway — five? With me and the wife, that'll make seven. Heh-heh-heh-heh-heh."

With that, the jet nosed skyward over the crowded, hustling metropolis of New York and twisted westward. I felt genuinely glad to be returning home to Kansas. Er, Missouri.

Everything's
up to date in
Kansas

A view from Hayward's Pit Bar-B-Que . . .

Here, perched on a knoll in southern Overland Park, Kansas, the sleekest barbecue restaurant you'll ever see caters to a corporate clientele and a neighborhood so "corporate" that even the family dogs wear three-piece suits.

Hayward's restaurant is the kind of place where the windows are smoked like the beef and the waitresses caper across carpets not yet stained with sauce or cigarette ash.

Ah, the newness of it all here on the College Boulevard strip! This is the Executive Corridor.

Only along the Executive Corridor could you find a barbecue restaurant, indeed an entire district, where someone once mused, "If only I had it to do all over again . . ." and did.

From scratch, the corridor was built so that everything would be taken care of. Nice homes for the families. Shops to clothe and feed them. Offices so they could earn their daily bread nearby. Trees and fields to inspire them. Banks, hospitals, schools.

Even a barbecue restaurant, so they could share a little part of Kansas City life — even if they just moved here from Phoenix.

And many of them have just moved here.

Kansas City is known as a regional headquarters town, where many large companies locate their Midwestern operations. Some of these, as well as home-grown concerns, have joined a migration from the Missouri side to the Kansas side. This migration is the lifeblood of the Executive Corridor.

Statistics are not thoroughly reliable, but one study estimated that by 1977 the number of businesses in Kansas City, Missouri, had declined 22 percent over 10 years. Another study showed that in the 1970s roughly 100 large companies (that use 10,000 square feet or more) had slipped over from Jackson County, Missouri, to Johnson County, Kansas.

With businesses on the move, and with residential neighborhoods already springing up in Johnson County, the creation of office parks and additional amenities along College Boulevard seemed only natural, perhaps inevitable.

Hence the lovely view through the smoked north windows of Hayward's barbecue . . .

The view embraces fabulously valuable real estate that sweeps through wood-shingled subdivisions and mammoth shopping centers and then disappears over a far ridge.

Nowhere in sight is the skyline of Kansas City, that ancient metropolitan center where executives used to work and play. No, the city and its problems are blotted out by an accommodatingly close horizon.

Seated in Hayward's, it is easy to forget the problems that besiege Kansas City: The declining downtown, the inner-city decay, the eroding tax base, the pressing need for capital improvements and the scarcity of funds to pay for them, the schools, the declining population.

In a Kansas City barbecue restaurant — Bryant's, for instance — it would be hard to forget those things. They seem to permeate the air.

For a Kansas Citian, it is painful to observe the Executive Corridor in Overland Park, to see a place constructed from scratch, exempt from the ravages of time. In the corridor, they have indeed had it to do all over. The leaders of the exodus talk about the productive labor, better schools and favorable tax structure in Kansas; the Missourians, angered, counter with their own arguments and rally to attract new businesses while hoping to retain the old.

Yet it seems the new Kansans can have their barbecue and eat it, too.

Surely, somewhere in this complex of low-slung buildings with tinted windows there is a catch. Isn't there a fatal flaw in the idea that you can leave your troubles behind, can desert the past and run to a miracle promised land? You can't really start over, can you?

Sure you can. No doubt, the land speculators and developers of 1880 believed they were starting over, as they began carving up the bluffs overlooking the Missouri and Kansas rivers. J.C. Nichols surely believed he was starting over when he built the Country Club Plaza 40 years later, miles to the south.

The Executive Corridor is simply the newest fresh start. In time, another will be required.

Suffering
yet another dig at
KC

Human suffering doesn't sell tickets in Kansas City.

— Woody Allen

This is a rather broad statement that, while probably dead right, deserves to be bashed against the wall a few times to see if it will bounce back.

The remark is heard in Woody Allen's latest film, "Stardust Memories." Like most of Woody's movies, it is about Woody, his pain, his torment and his inability to comprehend the world outside the boundaries of Area Code 212.

The hero of the film, Sandy Bates (played by Woody, of course), is a film maker whose people keep telling him not to make depressing films, as he is inspired to do, but instead stick with the funny ones that were so boffo at the box office.

The hero's people are especially disturbed by his latest film, which ends with two train loads of people meeting morosely at a garbage dump somewhere outside New York City. To the film maker, this garbage-dump rendezvous says it all about social relationships, existential gloom and "human suffering."

Which inspires one of his people to say, "Human suffering doesn't sell tickets in Kansas City." Of course, here in Kansas City, everybody chokes on their popcorn when this line is uttered. I am no different, and in fact, can't hear the ensuing dialogue because of it.

I think what follows is, "They've been working in the wheat fields all day," or something like that.

As it happened, everybody in the theater had been working in the wheat fields all day, and so we all nodded knowingly at this remark while brushing excess bran from our overalls.

When the film was over, I leaned back in my reclining seat to ponder it all. What had Woody Allen meant when he wrote, "Human suffering doesn't sell tickets in Kansas City"? I came up with a few ideas while watching the credits roll down and the wheat farmers walk out.

In the first place, Woody could just as easily have said, "Human suffering doesn't sell tickets in Tulsa" or Indianapolis or Topeka or Omaha or any one of a dozen American cities that to the East Coast mind connote the great "out there." You know, "out there," where people live on farms, where the Great Plains stretch out in an unending tableau of cows and trees, catfish and drive-in dairy bars.

And yet Woody chose Kansas City as his symbol for the great "out there." He did this, I feel certain, because of the song "Kansas City" ("I'm going to Kansas City; Kansas City here I come"). I may be wrong, but I think this song — more than the GOP convention in '76 and more than the sports teams — is responsible for Kansas City occupying shelf space in Woody Allen's brain. I admit I have no evidence for this theory.

But I suggest, nevertheless, that for many of the East Coast ilk Kansas City is the symbol of a vast Midwestern mystery. This mystery is not so much a whodunit but a whydotheylivethere. Woody Allen thinks of Kansas City and the region it represents as a continent of clods who are good only for growing wheat and, on Saturday night, for buying tickets to his movies.

Moreover, according to Woody, Kansas City has no appreciation for the one great subject of film: human suffering. "Human suffering doesn't sell tickets in Kansas City," the movie says. I can't get it out of my head.

Is this true? Doesn't human suffering sell tickets in Kansas City? I try to think of examples.

Immediately, the Kansas City Chiefs spring to mind. Here is a case of human suffering — on the part of the players and the fans — selling thousands of tickets in Kansas City.

Wrestling. There's another one. Wrestling is very big in Kansas City, Kansas, and those wrestlers must be suffering. They bleed and scream. Doesn't that count?

And George Brett. George was suffering for a while, and although ticket sales were brisk anyway, I'm sure his pain contributed to the desire for tickets.

Sitting here in my reclining chair, I realize that these are not very good examples of human suffering. Certainly, they don't compare with two trainloads of people meeting near a garbage dump outside New York City. Maybe Woody's right. Maybe human suffering doesn't sell tickets in Kansas City.

The thought depresses me. I suffer a little and then, reaching for my straw hat and pitchfork, I saunter out of the theater, just another farmer who wishes that Woody Allen would try to understand him better.

No More
Mister
Nice Guy

Kansas Citian Jimmy Green expressed it best: "It's so nice to be nice."

Who could argue? It surely is nice to be nice, especially in Kansas City.

Kansas City is a "nice guy" kind of a town. Everybody's nice to everybody else. Nobody seems quite able to bring himself to lambaste anyone.

Every time somebody goofs up or does something nasty, he gets an even break from folks around here. It happens all the time.

Last weekend Mike Livingston, the Chiefs' quarterback, heard only boos in the first half against the Cleveland Browns. He couldn't get the hometown club rolling. Substitute Steve Fuller came in and nearly won the ballgame.

Not surprisingly, newspaper columnists blistered Livingston for his performance and invited him to take a permanent place on the bench.

Many Kansas Citians — even some who had booed Livingston on Sunday — responded with, "Awww, they shouldn-a said that about Mike."

When Frederick Cross, former city attorney of Roeland Park, wrote that controversial memo suggesting that certain minorities be excluded from a first-offender program, many members of the white-collar set whispered among themselves: "Awww, he shouldn-a written that memo. That's not right."

But when Mexican-American protesters did their best to drive Cross from office in once-sleepy Roeland Park, the same folks could be heard saying, "Awww, they shouldn-a done that to Fred."

It's really hard to rile folks around here.

The Nazis arrived last year in the persons of two young swastika-wavers bent on turning KC into Berlin, 1936. They stomped, raved and got plenty of airtime on local stations and ink in the local press.

A few people were upset. But mostly Kansas Citians just looked on blandly, frowned gently, rolled their eyes a couple of times and ignored the poor zealots to death.

"Awww, they were just misguided," a few even said.

It's no wonder Ernest Hemingway left *The Kansas City Star* and went to war in Europe. He couldn't find anybody who'd duke it out with him in Kansas City.

It's the same way in politics. Take, for example, the philosophy of Jerry Jette, a political consultant. Jerry's the kind of guy who calls his friends "swine." But on the job he is smart enough never to inject his personal flair for name-calling into the public campaign tactics of his clients.

"In Boston, the more perverse or Machiavellian you are, the more they adore you," says Jette, gnashing his teeth. "In the Midwest, however, you can take a candidate's issues apart but you better be careful when it comes to his family or him personally."

Jette cited a recent example. Councilman Emanuel Cleaver, a newcomer to public office, attacked one of Mayor Richard L. Berkley's proposed appointments for the Housing Authority board, mortgage banker James Nutter. Cleaver pointed out that a banker might not make the most sympathetic administrator of public housing. Then Cleaver made the mistake of calling Berkley "stupid."

Around town, Berkley fans and non-fans could be heard to say, "Awww, he shouldn-a said that."

The point is that even Berkley's detractors, who call him everything from a stiff to a Republican shill, won't abide "stupid."

One of the few people in public life here who is always willing to get nasty is Tony DeHaro, ex-newscaster on Channel 5 and ex-host of "Kaleidoscope" on Channel 9. The reason Tony's been x-rated so often is that he has a sharp tongue, one that too often speaks the wicked truth. Why, Tony, is KC such a "nice guy" town?

"I credit it all to the fact that this is a very provincial community with a whale of an inferiority complex. In New York people want to know what you do, what you think. In Kansas City, the first question is always, 'How do you like Kansas City?'

"Kansas Citians are very protective of one another. They're afraid that if they acknowledge any faults they might be painted with the same brush. They say to themselves, 'This has to be utopia because I'm here and I'm never getting out.' "

Awww, Tony, you shouldn-a said that. On the other hand, maybe you should have. Much of it is true.

But so what? A little name-calling, a little nastiness is good for the soul of Kansas City. A boxer has to take punches if he wants to get near his opponent.

Perhaps the time has come when Jimmy Green's motto, "It's so nice to be nice," has outworn its usefulness. Maybe it's time to forsake caution and cure this city of terminal niceness.

To get the ball rolling, here's a clever slur received by this columnist in the mail recently. Michael Kobe of Olathe writes, in reference to a story on private security guards:

"Each day that your shining erudite face appears in my newspaper, I am assured of yet another example of journalism at its worst."

Thanks Mike. Stick it in yer ear.

See? That was easy. The road to thick skin may be paved with blisters. But it's a road worth traveling.

IDOLS
AND
IDOLATERS

All for a
Kiss
from
Liz

For denizens of Mission Hills, getting to see Liz was a simple matter of perfecting that coiffure and driving the Caddy a few blocks down the road.

But for Don Goodman, realizing the lifelong dream of meeting Liz Taylor meant weaseling out of a day's work at the aircraft factory in Wichita, hopping a bus and coughing up 40 hard-earned bucks to attend a political fund-raiser.

Goodman, 19, had heard Liz was to be in Kansas City to help raise funds for her husband, Sen. John Warner, R-Va., and Sen. Nancy Kassebaum, R-Kan.

Cringing with exquisite joy at the sight of Liz, Goodman said, "She's the most beautiful woman in the world. She could weigh 200 pounds and it wouldn't matter."

What a scene it was earlier in the afternoon. Where was Rona Barrett? Liz Taylor stepping off TWA Flight 183 totally unrecognized by the fast-moving airport crowd, looking tired on the arm of her tall, dark, Congressional hubby.

Whisked to the Alameda Plaza Hotel for a nap and two hours later a press conference with Warner and Sen. Kassebaum.

The three of them — the glamorous, raven-haired star of the silver screen, the dashing Virginia legislator, the Gentle Senator from Kansas and point-woman for the fair sex — are an all-star fund-raising team.

Goodman wasn't so concerned with the political clout, though, and focused hard on his idol, who was decked out in Halston sapphire blue "cocktail pajamas" and spiked heels.

While the press corps tried to plumb almost unfathomable depths of meaning at the conference, Goodman stood there in his rust-colored corduroy suit, his mouth wide open. Liz was explaining her Kansas "roots."

The short of it was her mother grew up on a Kansas farm. "It's sort of like coming home," obliged Liz. Sen. Warner grinned. The Gentle Senator smiled mysteriously.

It was almost like coming home, but actually it was more like raising money to pay off campaign debts.

Inside the gala reception at the Alameda, the trio formed a receiving line and shook the hand of every forty-dollar Bill who walked in, including Mr. Goodman. He had to stand in line for 20 minutes but it was worth it.

Shaking hands with Warner, he said, "I hope to see you in the White House." Liz recoiled visibly and said, "Don't say that, pllleeeze."

Next Goodman asked her if it would be OK to kiss her. It was. He did. As he sidled away from the line, Goodman rolled his eyes and gasped.

More than 300 passed through that line, many having their pictures taken with Liz Taylor and the two senators. Mayor Richard L. Berkley and his wife, Sandy, even got into the act. The mayor gave keys to the city to the celebs and kissed the ladies. Not to be outdone, Sandy Berkley smooched the Virginian.

Is this Kansas politics?

Ask Don Goodman; he has his finger on the pulse of this affair.

He thinks John Warner is presidential timber. The former secretary of the Navy looks like a president. And more importantly, Goodman notes, Liz would make a good First Lady.

He wonders why none of the reporters asked her about this. What a dream story it would be. From National Velvet to the national capital.

Since the age of 5, Goodman has followed her career. He's seen all her movies and has collected thousands of photographs of her. He knows almost everything there is to know about her. How old is Liz, Don?

"She was born Feb. 27, 1932, and has a brother named Howard. Is there anything else you want to know?"

She has a special magnetism that makes people want to touch her, he says. That's why she should be in the White House.

As Liz said herself at the press conference, politics and movies aren't so different. She has been a success at both.

The same quality that made her a star of the cinema has made her a star on the political fund-raising circuit. And that's where Liz Taylor meets Kansas politics.

The hordes who jammed her appearances at film premieres aren't so very different from the crowds who kiss her and shake hands at political functions.

Don Goodman may have hopped a bus out of Wichita to see Liz, drooled a bit when he did. But think about what went on inside the minds of the Mission Hills matrons who ogled that outfit, that husband, that power?

This is the wonderful thing about politics. It brings all sorts of people together.

Later in the evening Liz, her Virginian and the Gentle Senator would travel to a more exclusive fund-raiser to be attended by 50 couples who paid $500 each. Today they were to journey to Topeka to greet Sen. Kassebaum's father, former Gov. Alf M. Landon.

Don Goodman isn't sure what he's going to do. Maybe he'll follow the entourage, maybe he'll go back to his job at the aircraft plant. One thing is certain: He'll eventually go home a few dollars poorer, but richer for the experience of meeting Liz, of touching her sleeve.

Same goes for everyone who attended the political fund-raiser.

A
Beauty
To match the
Crisis

It certainly was gratifying to see a local girl, Miss Michelle Whitson of Mission, assume the mantle of Miss Kansas recently.

But, as pretty as she is, there are subtle changes afoot in this country that could compromise Miss Whitson's chances of becoming Miss America this September.

In the years past, of course, Miss America has been the very portrait of our nation. Her beauty, health, intelligence, talent and gentle poolside manner have been advanced as the highest ideals in the land.

Miss America *is* America in so many ways. And, like it or not, so is Bert Parks, with his wide, trusting grin and the beguiling gap between his teeth.

But that, remember, is the America of the past — the America of the Revolutionary War, Abraham Lincoln, John D. Rockefeller, Susan B. Anthony, Teddy and the Rough Riders, Eddie Rickenbacker, F. Scott Fitzgerald, FDR, Give 'em Hell Harry, rock'n'roll, *Life* magazine, the man on the moon and John F. Kennedy.

Those days are over. Jimmy Carter is president. we are in the midst of a "Crisis of Confidence." And that's why Michelle Whitson doesn't stand a chance of becoming Miss America.

The next Miss America, as she has strived to do in the past, must represent the true meaning and mood of the country.

After an exhaustive search along the highways and byways of this broad and gracious land, our talent scouts have found such a woman, an appropriate Miss America during this, our Crisis of Confidence.

They found her in a shack in eastern Colorado, where she lives with her daddy. Little Abbie Smith, at 18 years old, supports the family by working at a five-and-dime store in town. Ever since Dad's Winnebago dealership went bankrupt, she's held things together.

She stands only 5 feet 2 inches tall, a sliver of a girl with dark brown eyes and hair. Her eyes sparkle, though she is pale and her cheeks hollow with overwork and a diet of potatoes and candy from the store.

Dad sits at home most days shuffling his ledger books. Twenty years at the dealership have made him an optimistic man. There were all those sleek, power-drive homes he sold to all those happy, retired couples who wanted just to hit the road, and all those young families eager just to show their children the Heart of America.

Our scouts walked in on this scene recently and, taken by the poignant plight of this American pair, put Abbie through the motions of vying to be . . . Miss America (during our Crisis of Confidence).

Abbie's slight figure proved to be her first plus. The bathing suit competition, as you know, has been dropped from the contest and the Rag Bundle competition substituted for it.

Aglow with anticipation, Abbie gathered together all the rags her modest household had to offer and tied them around herself, bundling up well against the cold of an imaginary winter. At the contest in Atlantic City this September, all the girls will do the same.

Contestants will be judged for these qualities: Figure (do the rags fill her out in the right spots?), Poise (does she retain a semblance of dignity?) and Craftmanship (do the rags stay in place as she shuffles about the stage in her house slippers?).

Abbie was exquisite. "I feel so, so warm," she giggled.

Next the talent show, and here's where Abbie and her dad make such a great couple. He sat down at the old player piano and, pumping the pedals gaily, led Abbie in a rousing rendition of "Brother, Can You Spare a Dime?," a tune he remembers from the Great Depression when he was just a boy.

Abbie wowed our scouts with the way she sang the song, leaving her mouth slightly ajar all the way through. She looked really hungry. Dad was pleased and said, "Atta girl, things are gonna be OK!"

But the biggest test lay ahead. Those contest judges in Atlantic City will see a lot of girls with nice, skinny figures. They'll hear a lot of pitiful songs. Many a moon-faced girl will look their way.

The test this year to see who will be the next Miss America (during our Crisis of Confidence) will depend an awful lot on her coolness under the spotlight. This year, as in years past, Miss America contestants will be asked that Tough Question.

Impersonating Bert Parks, our scout gaped, "All right, Abbie, here's the big one. Are you ready?"

Abbie smiled and shuddered imperceptibly. Dad looked on nervously, his fingers plying the worn and tattered pages of a ledger book.

"Here's the question: You're at home alone in the middle of winter. It's 20 below outside and you run out of coal for the stove. It's snowing and you can't get out of the house. What can you do?"

"Oh, umm . . ." Abbie's eye skittered back and forth. She drew a deep breath, bent over a couple of times, then blurted out, "Freeze to death?!"

Isn't she marvelous?

When Bert Parks belts out the familiar, "Here she comes, Miss America" next September, it could be little Abbie Smith shuffling down the runway as Miss America (during our Crisis of Confidence).

He
Remembers
The
Nose . . .

So Jimmy Durante is dead. The guy with the big schnozzola, the "hot cha," the cigar and the face like pasta. What an old guy! Up by the bootstraps from the streets of New York, he soared to the pinnacle of show biz glory. His magic carpet was a nose and a lot of style. I was lamenting his passing, sitting at my desk.

Next thing you know, who should show up but one of Jimmy's old buddies, Charlie Stark. Charlie sidled up to the desk and said, "Oh, Jimmy Durante, what a guy!" We comistulated together. Pretty soon Charlie was telling me who he was and how he knew Jimmy. We covered a few other subjects, besides. It was deluminatin'.

"Jimmy Durante came out of my neighborhood — or I came out of his," explained Charlie, who is 70. "It was the Lower East Side of New York City, a ghetto. It was a ghetto — Italian, Jewish people, you know how it is. His brother was a policeman on Lansing Street. His brother had a beat there — he was a rotund little fella.

"He was tough. I was 10-11 years old. What I remember about him was when Jimmy Durante made it big, everybody knew about it, you know. You know, Italian people!"

While Jimmy Durante was busy making it big, Charlie was busy running around the city making a living as a designer. He designed the interiors of nightclubs. He says they used to call him "Little Red"; he had a song-and-dance routine of his own, too.

Now his red hair is graying, though there's still plenty on top of his head.

"In Prohibition days, they would confiscate everything. So the owners used to beg me to design the clubs in such a manner that . . . in the vernacular of the street in those days, the guys 'in the know' would know when a pinch was pending . . . So we just rolled up the joint — carpets, drapes, everything, my murals I painted, those little pieces of molding. I'd take 'em off right away.

"Anyway, this is not a story about me . . . We'd be sittin' around these speak-easies and Jimmy Durante would drop in and it wouldn't be long before some joker in show business would say, 'Hey, lend me $100 or $500.' If Jimmy didn't have it, he'd make Eddie Jackson get it for him. He had to give away at least $3 million to guys in the business who needed it."

Back in those days, Durante had a pretty big hit with the show "Strike Me Pink," and Charlie remembers a strange story involving the roadshow version. This show featured James Barton in Durante's role and a walk-on bit for Stark.

"Now Jimmy Barton was one of the 10 best dancers in the business, softshoe like Lou Clayton. But he would sing, he was a tremendous comic. All I know about him, he never had a nose."

Jimmy Durante's stand-in didn't have no nose?

"Jimmy Barton always had a hole — right here. I never questioned him. In those days, it wasn't days of plastic surgery. Today, you would have got a new nose. So he was always the first one in the theatre and the last to go. Even when he played Kansas City, he used to always have people roll in kegs of beer and coffee. He never left, 'cause he wanted to keep that putty nose on.

"He never left the theater, but when he left the theatre with his wife, myself — no nose — he was dapperly dressed, dapperly dressed. He was a dapper man, slender, always with the suede shoes. Even without the nose, he looked attractive. And we used to maybe go to a coffee shop and the tales I used to listen to! All that stuff. That's how I know so much about Jimmy Durante, how he would be so benevolent. He was always helping somebody."

After leaving the roadshow that starred the noseless stand-in for the Schnozz, Charlie came to Kansas City, where he made a reputation for himself as a designer. He designed the Inferno on Troost, Gigi's Lounge on Baltimore and numerous other places. He also designed some razzle-dazzle joints in Omaha, like The Twenties club.

"Now, gettin' back to Jimmy Durante. Last time I saw him was at Sam Nisi's Sparetime Cafe in Omaha. He musta been 75. He couldn't remember hardly anything, even his lines on TV. They used to make a joke of his forgetting his lines. They used to have fun with that.

"Anyway, I said to Jimmy, 'Jimmy, I've had this picture of you for a long time.' Look here."

It was a picture of Durante as a young man with chipped teeth, a little like Charlie's, a full head of hair and the Nose.

"I said go ahead and write, 'To my pal, Charlie.' So he writes, 'Solly.' "

What a disappointment! Oh well, it doesn't matter that much anymore. What with the perambulations of a whole career and the gesticulative motion of the Earth, not to mention Jimmy's ultimate passing. What's the difference between "Charlie" and "Solly"?

"Yeah," said Charlie and then he walked out. He's a better man for having known Jimmy Durante. Ain't we all?

. . . but the
Nose
forgot
him

Charlie Stark dropped by the newsroom the other day, as he is wont to do whenever some big star of stage and screen has died or recently passed through town. Charlie knows 'em all. He's available for interviews.

Charlie sits down and leans in close to make sure you get his stories right. An unlit, half-smoked cigar is an ever-present prop. He tawks kinda like dis, a displaced New Yorker who found his way to Kansas City before the last big war.

When Charlie was a kid on the Lower East Side, he made a name for himself as "Little Red," a scene-painter and all-around bit-part player in the vaudeville houses. He was a little guy, a "hoofer," but very willing, and in his early days he met some big-name types.

"Charlie Stark," he announces, cigar aloft, "friend of racketeers, stars and the little guy."

Charlie's 71 years old now. The red hair is graying. But the voice is still hearty and the memories are intact. The only problem, says Charlie, is that frequently when he reminds some big star or other about their friendship back in New York in the '20s, the star doesn't remember Charlie.

That's the way it was with Jimmy Durante, the "hot cha" guy with the cigar and the big nose. Charlie ran into Durante a number of years ago at Sam Nisi's Sparetime Cafe in Omaha. But Durante couldn't remember anything.

Durante signed a photograph for Charlie, but he wrote, "To my pal, Solly."

Same thing with Cab Calloway. Cab was in Kansas City this summer for a show at the Starlight Theater. Charlie figured he'd meet up with Cab at the Alameda Plaza Hotel and remind him of the good old days at Molly Picon's Second Avenue Theater.

There was that time when Cab brought a bevy of beautiful babes with him to the theater for a week-long stand. Eddie Rector and the Missourians were playing backup. All week long they sang and danced and the vaudeville fans went wild. But on Saturday night before the show — the time when vaudeville performers traditionally were paid — the manager was not forthcoming with the money.

Charlie watched it all from backstage, where he was pulling ropes (between acts he ran the silent flicks, too, because the projectionist was so old he fell asleep all the time).

Anyway, Cab didn't get his dough, so he screamed at his girls, "Hey, we're packin' it up. Let's get cabs. Let's get the heck outta here."

The show didn't go on. The patrons rushed to the box office to get their money back. But 55 years later in Kansas City, Cab had forgotten all about it.

"I reminded him of this, but maybe he didn't want to hear it in front of all those people at the Alameda," says Charlie, with regret in his raspy voice.

. . . Oh, yeah, and there was that time 12-13 years ago in Omaha, a city where Charlie has designed a number of nightclubs. At that time, Charlie was trying to get approval to start up a new nightclub called Diamond Lil's, which was named after Mae West's famous play.

But Mae, who died Nov. 22, wouldn't let him do it. Charlie told Mae's lawyer, "Tell Mae I was backstage when they were pinching her. She called me 'Little Red.' Tell her I'll give her royalties."

No dice. It was doubly irritating to Charlie because, he says, "There was a little dump in Des Moines called Diamond Lil's and she didn't object to that."

The whole idea was probably futile from the start, Charlie explains, because Sister Alice from the nearby College of Saint Mary didn't want Charlie's club in the neighborhood anyway.

. . . Oh, yeah, and there was old George Raft, who hung out in the New York vaudeville clubs in the '20s and who died Nov. 24, just a couple of days after Mae.

"Georgie Raft, he was a sharp-looking guy, with his hair all slicked back," Charlie recalls, a little sentimental now. "The girls went wild over him. He was almost classified in New York as a gigolo. Women sponsored him. He was the fastest Charleston dancer in the city. Everybody loved him. Mayor Jimmy Walker loved him."

Pretty soon Georgie took up with big band leader Ben Bernie and became a star. Charlie came to Kansas City, where he designed some nightclubs and built the first oversized Easter Bunny on the Country Club Plaza.

But that's another story in the life of Charlie Stark, "friend of racketeers, stars and the little guy."

If Jimmy
could just
Hit
.400

If you've seen the film "2001: A Space Odyssey," you'll remember the scene in which the primitive ape-men stare transfixed at a towering monolith. The monolith is the first icon and has the power to transform.

In modern-day American society, we have had no such monolith to worship. There was no single icon upon which we could all agree. Until recently, that is.

Now we have George Brett. Batting .401 in the American League, working miracles with a wooden cylinder, Brett is an icon of flesh who has the power to transform. I know. I have seem Him. He is in the very process of molding diverse America into a single Will.

Groveling gladly at the feet of a man who can hit .400, we Americans are becoming a collective line drive hit sharply up the middle. We fly beyond the reach of the quick glove of communism, the diving stab of recession, the shoestring catch of Third World unrest. We are "on base" with liberty, justice and another percentage point on our average.

Astonishing, yes. And if the cameras hadn't captured the events of Tuesday, future historians might doubt that it all ever happened.

A silver bird that said "United States of America" on its side winged across Kansas City's industrial basin bound for a meeting with George Brett. Secret Service agents scurried across the apron setting up the necessary communications equipment.

George Brett stood near the runway, waiting. He had accepted this audience with the president. The president was late.

All around him, lower-echelon politicians paid homage. Some tried to hide their interest in Brett. Others blatantly sought his favor. They shook the right hand of the icon. They slapped him on the back, but not too hard. They joked. They were obsequious and they knew it.

And Brett just stood there. His strong jaw struck a westward-looking profile, with the city's skyline poised grandly in the background. He dressed casually — to distinguish himself from the lesser mortals who tried to look good in suits and ties and afternoon dresses.

Brett wore cowboy boots in the manner of John Travolta. His shirt was open at the collar. When the president of the United States finally stepped off the airplane, George had donned his stunning violet velour jacket.

The president was awestruck. Having previously shaken the hands of a mere governor and congressman, Jimmy Carter pumped the icon's majestic limb for all it was worth (a reported $1 million annually for the next five years).

Metaphorically speaking, George Brett threw out the first ball of the election season. The players hustled onto the field. On to Truman High School in Independence for a presidential town meeting!

The crowd at the high school was abuzz with excitement. Seated in a banner-hung auditorium, they spied a small commotion at the door. The governor of the state, Joseph Teasdale, strolled in. The crowd applauded, but not too much. Call it a ground ball to the shortstop. Easy out.

Then came the icon. A hysterical avalanche of cheers battered the auditorium with sound, the low rumbling of males overarched by the high pitched squealing of a hundred teenage girls. The Truman High School cheerleaders led the way. A home run.

"George Brett . . . George Brett . . George Brett . . . George Brett," they chanted in rhythmic adulation.

A Secret Service agent leaned over and told one of his colleagues, "I think Brett's more popular than the Old Man."

I leaned over and asked one of the cheerleaders what she cared about more: the presidential campaign or Geroge Brett's campaign to bat .400. She looked at me, uncomprehending at first. Then she said slowly, and with great feeling, "George."

Oh, and yes, the president spoke. He talked of war and peace, energy and inflation, Ronald Reagan, the Russians, God and country. Everyone listened closely. It was nice. It was a national experience.

And when the president said how wonderful it was to be here in the home of Bess and Harry Truman, the Kansas City Royals and George Brett, it was an almost religious experience.

As befits the appearance of any figure so towering as Brett, there was a protester on hand. Not everyone worships this man of wooden miracles. Wayne Morse, an inveterate demonstrator and iconoclast, does not.

"Oh, I'm sick of hearin' about George Brett!" he said, outside the high school.

Wayne Morse stood alone with his picket sign, as a silver bird whisked the president from the citadel of George Brett, icon of flesh.

GOP
Aces
Bomb
Way to Victory

In deference to the Ronald Reagan Hollywood legacy, the columnist today offers his analysis of the 1980 election in a rough script of the new film, "Dogfight Over D.C.," a true-life, harrowing story that stars you-know-who.

The film climaxes as Ronald Reagan, squadron leader of the new conservative majority, leads his band of happy aces into air battle with Jimmy Carter and his squadron of washed-up liberals and New South moderates.

Reagan: OK, boys, we're going in. Let's win one for the Gipper. We've got to get government off the backs of the American people. Squadron leader to Jerry Ford. Do you read me, Jerry?

Ford: Roger, Ron. I have Jimmy Carter in my sights. This time I'll get him.

Reagan: Squadron leader to Henry Kissinger. Are you with me, Henry? Over.

Kissinger: Roger, governor. It sure feels good to be back at the trigger. How about a Cabinet post after we cream these guys?

Reagan: We'll discuss it later, Henry. Squadron leader to George Bush. Where are you, George?

Bush: I'm here, boss. Just to your left. How we doin'?

Reagan: OK, boys, this is it. I've waited a long time for this one. Let's go in and plant a few. Remember: A recession is when your neighbor loses his job. A depression is when you lose yours. And recovery is when Jimmy Carter loses his.

In a moment, the skies over Washington are filled with smoke and the sight of flashing tracer bullets. It's a dogfight over D.C. Jimmy Carter and his squadron mates are wracked by short bursts from the guns of the Reagan forces. A camera close-up reveals that Carter is aging at the controls. Carter's ship is reeling as he orders his squadron to take evasive action.

Carter: Go left, boys. No, go right. No, go left, boys. Squadron leader to Pat Caddell. Squadron leader to Pat Caddell. Come in, Pat. Come in, Pat!

Caddell: Yessir, sir. What is it, sir?

Carter: What do your polls show, Pat? Am I winning or losing?

Caddell: Well, sir, I can't make any sense of these polls I've been taking, but those four F-15s on your tail don't look so good. You better gain some altitude, Mr. President, or you're gonna be dead meat.

Carter: How much do I pay you?

With the Carter forces in disarray, the Reagan aces draw close. Suddenly out of the eastern sky at 1 o'clock, another squadron of conservatives emerges from the clouds, guns blazing. It's Jerry Falwell with his Moral Majority and Terry Dolan with his National Conservative Political Action Committee. These guys have firepower!

Falwell: I'm a-comin' Governor Reagan. It's time to fire the great guns of righteousness. God is my co-pilot. Now where is that peanut farmer?

Terry Dolan: Take that, you rat. Take that, you rat. Publicly financed abortions, huh? Take that. Defense cuts, huh? Eat lead. Bureaucracy lovers.

George McGovern: I'm hit. (Smoke fills McGovern's cockpit as the senator plunges to his political death.)

Birch Bayh: They got me. I'm going down. Say goodbye to Indiana for me.

Frank Church: I've lost power.

Plumes of smoke rise from the Potomac as Reagan's new conservative majority swoops in for the kill. In the background, the Battle Hymn of the Republic competes with the chatter of machine-gun fire and the whooshing sounds of air-to-air missiles.

Carter (barely audible over the din): Ed Muskie? Ed Muskie, do you read me? I'm sorry, Ed. I'm sorry I got you into this. You should have stayed in the Senate, but I made you my secretary of state. Now you're going down, too. And Walter Mondale. Fritz, open your chute! Open your . . . Gee whiz. They're all gone.

The camera closes in on a strong, smiling, confident Ronald Reagan — a reasonable man directing a stream of hot lead toward the presidential fighter plane. Reagan looks great in leather.

Reagan: It's time for a new majority, Jimmy. This country's sick and tired of you and your kind. We've got to get rid of you so the American people can be free to do what I know they can do. So long, Jimmy (rat-a-tat-tat).

Bush: You got him. ATTA WAY TO GO!

With Jimmy Carter and his Democratic cronies erased from the sky, Ronald Reagan and the new conservative majority wing their way into the sunset. In the distance, their squadron is joined by hundreds and hundreds of aircraft pulling into a tight formation from every direction. It's a new majority. The dogfight over D.C. is finished.

Glory, glory hallelujah
Glory, glory hallelujah

Mayor honors
Rabbit
and other
Bigshots

There was a time when the key to the city was so big you had to carry it around on your shoulders. This was no ceremonial object. Centuries ago, townsmen of prominence could be seen lugging huge wooden keys that unlocked the gates to their fortified cities.

Today the tradition lives on in a watered-down sort of way. All over the world, mayors honor distinguished visitors with the key to the city. Bugs Bunny, for one, has a key to Kansas City.

"It just gets into how you define 'distinguished,' " notes Mayor Richard Berkley.

The key-to-the-city ritual is very much in evidence here. Since May 1979, the city has bought 1,000 of the small tokens from the company that makes them, the Green Jewelry Co. of Lenexa. The keys are about 1½ inches long, are of copper and gold plate and spell out "KC" where the teeth ought to be.

Berkley, who is the principal dispenser of the keys, says he can't recall dishing out all 1,000 of them and believes some are still "in the pipeline," meaning they haven't been readied for delivery around the necks of visiting dignitaries.

The mayor gives out the keys at the airport, at dinners in hotels, in government offices — virtually anywhere an honored personage from out of town is likely to be found. Most of the key giving is planned. If Berkley knows Sen. Howard Baker is going to be in town, as he was last November, the mayor packs a key to be hung around the senator's neck on a ribbon.

The mayor notes, however, that sometimes he doesn't know for sure whether giving a key is appropriate — sometimes it's preferable to say hello and smile. For this reason Berkley carries a key or two with him much of the time *just in case* he feels inspired to give one out.

The keys come in very handy for the mayor. He collects autographs, so when a famous person shows up in town, he gives the key and the celebrity gives an autograph — "in red," says the mayor, "because it shows up better."

Some celebrities who recently visited Kansas City and got the key are Elizabeth Taylor, Bruce Jenner, Art Linkletter, Clayton Moore (the Lone Ranger), Shana Alexander, Sally Kellerman, Jodie Foster, Lena Horne, Cab Calloway, Bugs Bunny and a lot more.

What with the constant flow of keys out of City Hall, it is hard to keep track of them all. Berkley has trouble recalling just what brought Bugs to town, for example. "He was here promoting *something* . . ." says the mayor, shaking his head.

In exchange for the key, Bugs passed out some fresh carrots that were well received around City Hall.

In addition to honoring visitors to the city, keys are good for handing out when the mayor visits another city or country. Many keys were issued on a recent trip to Japan. When Berkley went to New York City, he gave Mayor Ed Koch a key. Koch, who's always looking for a handout, accepted graciously and gave Berkley a necktie.

In a recent visit to Seattle, Berkley bumped into the mayor of Tainan City, Taiwan, which is one of Kansas City's five "sister cities." The mayor of Tainan City endowed Berkley with a large, shimmering gold key of very fine craftsmanship. Berkley admits to being slightly chagrined at having to reach for the little KC token, which comes in a plastic box and wholesales for $3.56 (not including the ribbon).

Speaking of the ribbon, there was the time one of the mayor's assistants cut the ribbon too short. The result: When Berkley went to place the key over a dignitary's head, the key nestled tightly around his forehead. This, as one might surmise, is not where the key to the city should be worn.

(The short ribbons were salvaged and used to adorn some of the various documents the city issues to honor dignitaries and locals who don't get the key to the city. These include Resolutions, Proclamations, Commendations and Certificates of Citizenship.)

In its original conception, the key was designed to be worn on a bracelet, as a tie-bar or on a necklace, or simply kept as a memento. It was L.P. Cookingham, city manager from 1940 to 1959, who decided he didn't like the looks of the old wooden key languishing in City Hall and resolved in 1942 that it was high time Kansas City had a modern key.

Since then, Cookingham and Berkley agree, there was one undisputed champion key giver, H. Roe Bartle, mayor from 1955 to 1963. A magnanimous man, Bartle was known to leave town with his pockets brimming with keys. He gave them to doormen and stewardesses.

It is not known whether he ever gave one to Bugs Bunny.

LAW
AND
DISORDER

A
Sense
of duty
Prevails

The date was June 15, 1975 — Father's Day. Jim and Shirley Petet were taking the kids to watch their son play little league baseball.

They were a typical Independence family on a typical suburban outing.

"Oh, mom, look, there's a car like Aunt Nancy's," their daughter said, pointing at a yellow 1966 Cadillac that crossed Noland Road in front of them.

It could have happened to anybody, really. A car crossing the street, a glimpse at a face, the sensation of something out of the ordinary, frozen in memory.

The Cadillac that looked like Aunt Nancy's made witnesses of the Petets. It drew them with sudden force from the tranquility of their everyday lives to the hammering finality of arrest and judgment.

It forced Shirley and Jim Petet to take the stand and share the burden of accusing a murderer.

As it happened that June 15, it was a 40-year-old Kansas Citian, Vincent X. Lee, who drove the yellow Cadillac across Noland and into the parking lot of a 7-Eleven store. Lee robbed the store of $219 and led Mrs. Judith Lynn Mitchell, the clerk, and Robert L. Pope, a customer, into the back room of the store.

Then, as they lay on the floor, Lee killed them with a fusillade of .22-caliber bullets to the head, neck and back. They were the fourth and fifth victims of the same gun within a matter of days, court testimony indicated.

While Lee snuffed out the lives of Mrs. Mitchell and Pope, the Petets hurried on to the baseball game. Their son's coach was a demanding one who enforced punctuality. They knew it was about 2 p.m. and they knew they were a little late.

When the family returned home a couple hours later a neighbor told them there had been a killing at the store and that a yellow Cadillac had been seen in the vicinity.

Jim and Shirley Petet said nothing to each other about the matter until after dinner. In their minds, though, they knew they had seen a yellow Cadillac.

That was the turning point, then, wasn't it? It was the moment when a person mentally acknowledges something, something unpleasant, and then chooses whether to bury it. Many do bury it. Fortunately, the Petets did not. They decided after dinner to make a report to the police.

They had no idea what they were getting into.

What followed was a series of interviews with police and prosecutors, trips to downtown Kansas City and Independence, appearances in court, questions by the media, lost days at work and with the family and, for Shirley Petet at least, a nagging fear that maybe she wasn't doing "the right thing."

The Petets weren't the only witnesses, of course. Others testified that Lee was the man they saw near the store. One witness placed him in the store, another saw him leave and then went in and found the bodies lying on the floor. None of these witnesses ever received intimidating phone calls, as did Katherine Jo Allen, the young rape victim who was killed recently, just before she was to take the stand in her assault case.

Yet when Shirley Petet testified in 1975, she sat 10 feet from Vincent X. Lee. That was intimidation enough, to look into his face.

It is no wonder that, after Lee was sent to jail, the Petets followed closely the news stories about Missouri's law granting women exemptions from jury duty. The stories told how that law was being contested in high courts. Jim Petet had a sinking feeling when he read in January of this year that the U.S. Supreme Court had ruled the law unconstitutional.

He learned from the newspaper that Vincent X. Lee would get a new trial.

Although reluctant, the Petets went through it all again with a new prosecutor. There were more trips downtown to the county courthouse, more interviews. Ultimately, they journeyed to Springfield, Mo., where the case was moved, and Shirley Petet lost two days' pay. She feared she would lose her job.

It was while the second Lee trial progressed that the news about the murder of Katherine Jo Allen reached the witnesses in the Lee case. At least one became very fearful, although the witness never had been threatened. The witness declined to be interviewed for this story, out of fear.

What motivates these witnesses, torn from their rather ordinary lives, to face the fear and swear before the court that, yes, I saw that yellow Cadillac and, so help me God, the driver looked like Vincent X. Lee?

A simple sense of duty.

For Jim and Shirley Petet, their years of association with the American Legion helped solidify that sense of duty. For others, duty is less clearly defined. It derives, perhaps, from the knowledge that there comes a time to stand up and be counted for something.

Katherine Jo Allen had that knowledge, but died before she got the opportunity to testify in court. The Petets had that knowledge and have been lucky enough to return, undisturbed, to their lives in Independence.

There's a
Moral
Here
Somewhere

This is a story with a moral. However, the moral is flexible and depends on how much you like people who drive big, expensive cars.

First the story — as related by Mr. Horst Schwab, who is the central figure and outraged party in this saga.

Mr. Schwab was minding his own business, driving his $55,000 Mercedes 6.9 black limousine in the area of the art museum early in the evening of Sept. 10. He had three passengers in the car, which was one of many Mercedes he owns as president and 100 percent owner of the Aristocrat Motor Co., 16th & Baltimore.

The president of Aristocrat Motor Co. was wending his way toward the Country Club Plaza when, in his rearview mirror, he spied an officer of the law following close behind.

Mr. Schwab believed himself generally innocent and could think of no charges outstanding against him — other than that he was driving a huge black limousine with dealer's license plates and a telephone antenna on the back.

As Mr. Schwab looked repeatedly in the rearview mirror, he began to sense an accusing finger following him on four wheels through the Plaza. The Aristocrat Motor Co. executive began to feel . . . *paranoid.*

Mr. Schwab was so nervous that he turned left before he ordinarily would have on his route to Ward Parkway. So it was in front of the swank Bristol Bar & Grill on Jefferson that the officer flashed his red lights and, as Mr. Schwab put it, "with considerable overkill also blasted his siren."

Mr. Schwab did not consider all that hoopla necessary, especially in front of a posh club on a busy Wednesday evening in the Plaza.

The car dealer waited in his Mercedes for two minutes, expecting the officer to announce the charge against him. When no such action was forthcoming, Mr. Schwab disembarked from the limousine and demanded to know the charge. The reply: "Sir, go back and wait in your car."

Mr. Schwab didn't like the tone of the officer's voice.

Five more minutes passed — lights still flashing in front of all the fashionable cocktail-drinkers — before Mr. Schwab was informed that he was being arrested for operating his personal car with a dealer's license plate.

Mr. Schwab was outraged. He explained that yes, this was his car — just as all the cars owned by Aristocrat were his. But the car was not being used for personal purposes.

Moreover, he argued, how could the officer possibly know for what purpose the car was being used? And furthermore, how could this officer arrest him for using a dealer's plate when every dealer in town does the same? (Indeed, the city code against using dealer's plates for personal driving is rarely enforced.)

For a full 25 minutes, the big Mercedes waited in front of the bar. Mr. Schwab grew livid. He imagined, "Everybody on the Plaza at seven in the evening saying, 'What is going on here? . . . Oh, look at that big Mercedes, wonder who he raped today?'

"What the hell? I'm a criminal or something?"

After giving himself three days to cool down, the president of the Aristocrat Motor Co. wrote the chief of police a letter expressing his outrage. Here is the highlight of that letter, a copy of which was sent to *The Kansas City Times:*

"This humiliating intrusion and insult, made more offensive by the contemptuous attitude and tone of voice, made more dramatic by the senseless blasts from his siren, made more humiliating by his choice of places to stop and by the uninterrupted flashing of red lights, and made more unforgivable by continuing the harassment for 25 minutes, is the most outrageous offense I have ever experienced as an American citizen.

"I now understand discrimination beyond race, color and creed. There can also be discrimination against expensive cars . . ."

So where, dear reader, is the moral? Are we to take pity on poor Mr. Schwab — whose $55,000 Mercedes caused him that excruciating embarrassment upon the Plaza? Right there in front of the Bristol Bar & Grill?

Or should we take up the cause of the officer in question? Is he a working man's hero — a man who dared confront the Aristocrat Motor Co.'s finest automobile and chief officer? Did he, in humiliating Mr. Schwab, strike a blow for every poor slob who drives a Volkswagen? An aging Chrysler? Yea, even a rusted-out Saab?

You figure it out.

(Postscript: Manfred Maier, the Police Department attorney, says the department has asked that the dealer's plate charge be dropped and adds, "Somebody will talk to the officer.")

Salesman Died
at His Trade

Al Applebaum lived and died a salesman.

Selling low-cost shirts and shoes to the poor, extending credit and collecting on the weekends, locking the door and admitting only regular customers to a cluttered store at 35th and Prospect, that was Al Applebaum's working life.

But he liked it. He was 68 years old. He knew all that came with the territory.

And when someone thrust a pair of scissors countless times into Al's body last Saturday afternoon, that came with the territory too. It wasn't the first attack.

Five years before, a robber had beaten Al over the head with a gun butt, opening a wound that later required 200 stitches. When the gunman moved toward the cash register, Applebaum grabbed him and dragged him over the counter. Police arrived on the scene and shot the robber.

Why didn't Al quit then, while he was ahead?

The salesman began his career as a newspaperboy on the streets of Louisville, Ky. His father had brought the family to America when Al was just 8 years old.

Because his father couldn't find steady work Al was forced to drop out of school in the eighth grade and learn at an early age how to hustle a buck.

Besides newspapers, he peddled ice cream at the Churchill Downs race track. As a young man Al earned some money as a semi-professional football player with the Shawnee Knights in Louisville.

Al returned to the life of a salesman after war took him to the Philippines and peace brought him to Kansas City. His first years here were as a meatcutter, but by the 1950s Al had married and joined his father-in-law, Jake Kurash, in the clothing business.

They sold clothes out of the trunk of a car for years and eventually opened the J & A Outlet on 12th street. They moved the store twice in succeeding years, first to 27th and Prospect and then to 35th and Prospect, where the operation became known as Al's Outlet.

Why didn't Al quit while he was ahead?

As proprietor of Al's Outlet, Al was like a lot of other merchants who chose to stick it out along Prospect. Their stores were their livelihoods. The neighborhood was familiar and, as often as not, they were in debt to the bank.

Al knew everybody in the neighborhood, knew when they would be needing clothes and sold them the merchandise even if they were low on funds.

Al saw the effects of poverty on Near East Side residents and saw their dependence on government checks. His business ebbed and flowed with the arrival of the checks. But he never became cynical about it.

The riots of 1968 hit hard at Al's Outlet. The storefront windows were shattered and his inventory looted. But like other merchants who suffered the same fate, Al had a stake along Prospect. He wasn't about to move. His friends recall that he took the setback in stride and bore no grudge.

Al and his wife, Ida, had two sons, Richard and Victor, and both learned young how to sell. Al took Victor, at age 7, in the family car and let the boy peddle gloves and other work items to service station workers, just to give Victor the feel of working.

Now the two sons are salesmen, too, and have nice homes and families. They haven't had to struggle quite like their father did. Al saw to that.

By the time Al reached his 60s his family was urging him to retire to his modest home in south Kansas City. His sons were earning money, they argued, and Al could afford to slow down.

But he wouldn't do it. After a lifetime of jawing, traveling and hustling for a living, he didn't know how to quit.

So he stayed on. He kept on running that little shop. On weekends he'd make the rounds, collecting debts. He helped people find a lawyer if they needed one, told them who to talk to about tax problems. He became a kind of informal mayor of 35th and Prospect.

He liked to feel needed.

After he was beaten, Al started locking the door, opening it only for his regular customers. But as he grew cautious, he did not grow vengeful. He never kept a weapon on the premises.

Why didn't Al quit while he was ahead?

After the attack, Al referred to himself as "semi-retired." But he went to the store seven days a week. Sticking to a lifelong pattern, he didn't take vacations and worked every Sunday, even if only for a few hours.

It was sometime between 1 p.m. and 6 p.m. Saturday afternoon that someone gained entrance to Al's Outlet and killed him. Police found signs of a struggle but apparently no indication that a robbery had taken place.

Along Prospect, the merchants shake their heads, in grief but not in surprise.

Why didn't Al quit while he was ahead? Because he never was ahead. He made a living on discount merchandise and conversation. And he needed customers.

Fast
Bike is King's
Undoing

For Gerald "Swede" Peterson, the most familar sound of all was a police siren to his rear; the most familiar sight, a roadblock ahead. He screeched, swerved, rammed and busted through life.

And when his time ran out Tuesday, there were a lot of cops who shook their heads, recalled for a moment the King of the Chase and then closed the file on Swede Peterson.

He could have made a great race driver. But his track was the city street, the highway. There was something about Swede, a 48-year-old country boy from outside St. Joseph, that made it impossible for him to resist a car chase with police officers. There probably were more than a hundred.

Some said the police goaded him into the chase. Others said he goaded the police. Whichever way it was, it was "a matter of principle" for both sides.

Back in the 1960s, when Swede was in his driving prime, he'd be chased every night of the week, according to Capt. Bob Collins of the Independence Police Department. On the average Peterson would get away 14 out of 15 times. He was that good.

He'd get away because if a police officer couldn't get a positive identification on him there was little chance of a conviction in court — it wasn't enough just to get a license number.

"I truly believe that if you put him on the pole in the Indy 500," Collins would say after Swede met his demise, "and put a set of lights and a siren on his trunk, he'd win easily."

Swede's career as a roadrunner had two high points, two eras in which his name was emblazoned on police reports and newspaper stories by the dozen.

There was the famed North Kansas City chase in 1966. Peterson was observed squealing his tires at 18th and Swift and police gave chase. Swede whooshed out onto I-29 after evading the first roadblock and sideswiping two cars. On I-29, he lost control of his car and spun into the oncoming lane, scattering cars this way and that.

Police lost him briefly, but gave chase minutes later in a residential district as Swede headed for the Paseo Bridge. A roadblock there forced him to spin around into the wrong lane again and cops started to shoot. He got away again.

Then a Kansas City police officer spotted him on Armour and followed him into the Northeast Industrial District at speeds up to 100 miles an hour. One more roadblock later, Swede crashed into a light pole and took off on foot. They caught him on a porch and issued him a fat ticket for 44 traffic violations.

Upholding his reputation for a willingness to "run right out of his shoes," Swede led the police on another wild chase two weeks later, again in North Kansas City. This time policemen responded to a burglary call and found Swede's car with the keys in it at the scene. They waited for him.

Peterson ran across the street and another police car smashed into a light pole, swerving to avoid hitting him. Swede got in his car and took off while officers emptied their guns at his car. Peterson ditched the car and escaped on foot.

The scene was reminiscent of the time Swede led one officer on foot into a backyard and "clotheslined him" — ran him right into a clothesline and dumped him. It also recalled the time in Clay County when officers looked on in astonishment after every piece of glass in Swede's car was shattered by gunfire and he emerged from his demolished car unhurt.

Things finally caught up with Swede in 1968 and federal authorities packed him away for almost 10 years in the federal penitentiary on burglary and narcotics convictions. His second high-point came in the last month.

About three weeks ago, Swede was driving his El Camino when Independence police spotted him and gave chase. During the sprint Peterson rolled his car and fled on foot. But he was captured. He was just warming up.

On Sept. 14, Kansas City policemen spotted him downtown and took off after the elusive Swede. The chase fired up when Highway Patrol officers clocked the King at 140 mph down Manchester Trafficway. A Lee's Summit patrol car was totaled in a wreck as Swede hurtled on.

Peterson ditched his car near 93rd and Westridge and ran. Police dogs, helicopters and police officers scoured the area. They found him in a clump of woods.

On Tuesday, Swede did something police had never seen him do before — he sped through a radar trap on a motorcycle. He had always done his high-steppin' in a car. The chase was over the minute Swede cut into the wrong lane of traffic on Blue Mills Road and plowed into a pickup truck at 80 mph.

The King was dead.

In the aftermath, his longtime Kansas City lawyer, Robert Duncan, recalled Swede as "a hell of a nice guy, generous," a guy who occasionally was struck by the desire to go straight but couldn't overcome his past.

The police — the men who jammed their accelerators to the floor to catch him — remembered Swede simply as the King.

Is
Willie
Really a
Rat?

Underworld mobsters, while no great contributors to the betterment of society, do provide the rest of us with some diversion from the drone of daily life.

They murder, skim, extort and speak colorfully to each other over wiretapped phone lines. We read all about it in the newspapers.

Some people enjoy this diversion. Others think only a moral defective could gain any pleasure from the exploits of gangsters.

All will agree, at least, that mobsters and alleged mobsters do make one very positive contribution to society — their nicknames.

Mobsters' nicknames are an important part of the folklore of crime. A good number of history's most heinous crooks had them. Al "Scarface" Capone, George "Machine Gun" Kelly, Charles "Pretty Boy" Floyd, to name just a few.

A lot of modern-day crime figures are tagged with flashy nicknames as well. William "Willie the Rat" Cammisano, Anthony "Tony Ripe" Civella, Carl "Tuffy" DeLuna are some local fellows whose names catch the eye.

Where do all these nicknames come from? Do the mobsters like them? What would happen if you should bump into Anthony Accardo and call him by his nickname, "Big Tuna"?

The nicknames, according to law officers and reporters, derive from a variety of origins. Some are childhood names that stick. Others are street names that are descriptive of a man's "territory," his character or his appearance. Still others begin as code names, used between gangsters to maintain security.

Some nicknames are probably endowed by the press. Most are strongly supported by the press. The reason for this is simple: Nicknames make flashy copy.

Take, for instance, the story of Tony "Lollypop" Mangiaracina, a crook who was executed in 1930 for the murder of Kansas City police officer James "Happy" Smith. Headlines during the trial read: "Jolt To Lollypop"; "A Lollypop Alibi"; "Lollypop To Die" and "Lollypop Has No Fun."

Lollypop, by the way, cracked jokes on his way to the gallows.

The nicknames are not necessarily a laughing matter. "Willie the Rat" Cammisano, for example, has taken umbrage publicly at one story of how he got his nickname.

Fred Harvey Bonadonna, at a congressional hearing on organized crime, explained that William Cammisano "was called Willie The Rat becaused he killed people and stuck them in the sewers so the rats could get them."

To the contrary, William Cammisano explained, the name was really "Willie Rats," which he got because his rat terrier Trixie used to kill rats in the neighborhood stores back when the Kansas Citian was a kid.

Some nicknames are controversial, like William Cammisano's, but are not the subject of dispute.

For example, Joseph "Joey Doves" Aiuppa, a Chicago gangster, acquired his nickname in 1962 after a hunting trip in southeast Kansas. Federal wildlife officers discovered 500 mourning doves packed away in the Chicagoan's car trunk, some 476 above the legal limit. The slaughter was called one of the biggest game law violations in American history.

"Jimmy the Weasel" Fratianno, whose story is told in Ovid Demaris' book *The Last Mafioso,* was named Aladena by his parents but he considered the name too effeminate. He started calling himself "Jimmy." One day, at the age of 11, he hit a policeman in the face with a rotten tomato and, while he was running away, a bystander remarked, "Look at that weasel run!" The moniker stuck.

These nicknames are not always popular with their owners. As Tom Renner, an organized crime reporter for *Newsday,* points out, "You wouldn't call Tony Accardo 'Big Tuna' and expect to go on living." (The name, by the way, comes from a large fish the gangster once caught.)

No, in general, you would be wise to call some of these fellows — those who are still living — by their given names:

Benny "The Bum" De Martino (a poor dresser). Morris "Snag" Klein (aggressive teeth). Carmine "The Snake" Persico (a deceiver who led Larry Gallo into a failed murder trap). Angelo "Charlie Four Cents" Salerno (always short on cash). Johnny "Coca-Cola" Lardiere (a man who really liked "The Real Thing").

Not to mention Mateo "Shopping Bags" Cuomo (who collected debts in grocery sacks) and Dominic "Swats Mulligan" Ciffone (who practiced the art of persuasion with a baseball bat).

And many, many more, of course.

No matter what you may think about the bad guys, you have to give them credit for one thing — they invariably manage to improve on their birth certificates.

He's against
Gum
Control
on his block

The unruly weeds near Dr. James Bridgens' Ward Parkway-area home grow in silent protest to one of Kansas City's lesser-known laws: Never plant a sweet gum tree on a red maple street.

Bridgens, well-known for years as deputy coroner for Johnson County, made the mistake of planting a sweet gum tree on a red maple street and, now that the "authorities" have dealt with the situation, Bridgens is hopping mad.

"I think it is a violation of my personal rights!" he says.

Pitted against Bridgens in the dispute is Beatrice Davis, wife of former Mayor Ilus Davis and currently the vice president in charge of islands and parking greens for the Country Club District Homes Association.

Says Mrs. Davis of her neighbor, "This seems to have driven him to a frenzy."

The story begins three years ago when an elm tree died in the parking strip along Bridgens' property at 1025 Huntington Road. Bridgens and his wife observed that the death of the elm left a vacancy in the strip. So two years ago they planted a sweet gum tree to replace it.

Bridgens felt free to do as he wished with the parking strip because he had maintained it himself since moving to the house in 1961. Moreover, Bridgens had invested in a sprinkler system to "make it look nice."

Last summer, the pathologist took special care to nurture the little sweet gum. He watered it frequently to counteract the ferocious heat and drought. The tree seemed to be doing well but, alas, it was doomed. You see, it was a sweet gum on a red maple street.

One day during the summer, Bridgens recalls, Beatrice Davis was passing by and remarked to him, "My, what a lovely little maple!" And, says Bridgens, "I made the fool mistake of telling her it was a sweet gum."

Some months later, after returning from a vacation around Thanksgiving, Bridgens came home from work and noticed that the sweet gum had been removed. A maple stood in its stead.

"My God," he said. "What happened to my tree?"

First, Bridgens called the city, thinking the park department was the culprit.

George Eib, superintendent of forestry and landscaping for the department, remembers the call: "He called me. He thought it was the city. Man, he read me the riot act."

Further investigation, however, revealed that the Country Club District Homes Association had the tree replaced. The Rosehill Gardens Nursery, acting on instructions from the association, had moved the sweet gum four blocks away to Belleview.

Mrs. Davis explains the move: "The tree he planted was a sweet gum in what otherwise is a maple block. We moved the sweet gum tree to Belleview, which is the street that is sweet gum."

Mrs. Davis further explains that, since Dutch elm disease ravaged the city's elm population in the late '50s, the city has had a plan that specifically designates what species of tree is to be planted where. This is done to prevent a single disease from wreaking widespread destruction again.

George Eib confirms that citizens wishing to plant trees in the parking strip areas must obtain a permit from the city and must plant the appropriate species. In other words, you can't plant a sweet gum on a red maple street. And vice versa.

Mrs. Davis' homes association has been very active in the planting of appropriate trees and has even raised association dues in order to foot the bill in some cases.

"Most of the people in our association are really happy with the tree program," Mrs. Davis notes.

Bridgens, however, is livid. "They've had the audacity to capriciously steal my own property," he asserts.

The pathologist has embarked on a two-pronged protest campaign against the tree-switching maneuver by the homes association. First, he recently traded written salvos with association officials and has refused to pay this year's dues. Second, he has stopped mowing the grass in the parking strip or picking up refuse there.

"I found an easy solution," says Bridgens. "Just let the stuff grow! It looks great, and it's good for the wildlife. My wife used to spend a lot of time clearing out the beer cans that collected there. Now you can't see 'em because of all that tall grass."

Mrs. Davis points out that letting the grass grow long in humid weather is likely to encourage diseases that will harm the grass in the future. But Bridgens has another reason for neglecting the parking strip: He doesn't want to be accused of molesting the new maple.

Says he: "God help me if I should accidentally kill the tree."

Dianna's
Hope
Dies
With Her

Her dreams were modest. Living with her family in a crowded household, Dianna Bunyan only wanted what her job at the restaurant and her husband could give her — sustenance and a child.

But Dianna's story ended early, very early. On Saturday, at the age of 18, she fell to the pavement with a mysterious ailment. Two hospitals sent her away, saying they couldn't do anything for her.

Her husband put her to bed Saturday night, her legs paralyzed, and she died in her sleep.

This is how it happened.

Dianna hired on as a counter girl at the Town Topic restaurant, 2801 Nicholson, more than two years ago to work the night shift. Her mother, Mrs. Earl White, had been working mornings there five years.

After her marriage to construction worker Christopher Bunyan, slightly more than a year ago, Dianna hoped to become pregnant as some of her friends had. But in the course of the year her hopes went unfulfilled.

Dianna's real troubles began in May when she started experiencing pains in her thighs. She went to a clinic at Truman Medical Center May 31 and was told her problem was her bulk. She weighed 261 pounds, and stood 5 feet, 7 inches tall. A pregnancy test proved negative.

She returned to the hospital two days later with the same complaint and after a routine examination and a kidney test, she was told to return to the clinic in two days.

But she didn't go.

Fatefully, the day she was supposed to be at the clinic, Dianna collapsed in the street while using crutches. She couldn't move her legs. Her husband called an ambulance and she was rushed to TMC.

A doctor in the emergency room there, after noting her symptoms and conducting a simple neurological exam, concluded that Dianna was exhibiting "bizarre behavior" and recommended she seek psychiatric evaluation at Western Missouri Mental Health Center.

Three weeks passed. Dianna, her husband and mother were shopping downtown Saturday when her legs gave out again. This time Dianna was taken by cab to TMC. The cab driver found a wheelchair and Dianna was wheeled into the emergency room.

Forms were filled out and she was asked to wait. According to her husband, they waited for "quite some time" before a nurse or clerk came into the waiting room and said, "Well, there isn't anything we can do."

Bunyan recalls the nurse's last words: "Now, don't steal our wheelchair."

Medical records simply state: "(She) apparently left before being evaluated."

After leaving TMC, Bunyan and a family friend took Dianna to the Osteopathic Center where essentially the same thing happened. A spokesman for that hospital said Dianna had told a staff member that she had just been at TMC.

"We really couldn't do any more for her than they did at TMC," the spokesman said. Dianna didn't have insurance or money and because the emergency room staff didn't see any emergency, she was sent away again.

Bunyan told a slightly different story. After being asked whether the couple had insurance, he recounted, "I said I didn't think so. They asked if I had $39 and I said no.

"Then another doctor came out and said, 'No, you got to have $39 to get into the room.' That's when he told me we should go to Truman Medical Center and we told him that's where we just came from."

Finally, Dianna was taken to the only place that would have her — the couch at home, 1610 Lister, where she lived with her husband, mother, father and three brothers and sisters. She lay there until 1:15 a.m. when she called out asking to be taken upstairs.

Dianna was taken up the stairs and put to bed. She could barely move.

"The last thing I did," recalls her mother, "I said goodnight and she said goodnight."

The next morning Christopher Bunyan found his wife dead in bed.

He had planned to take her to Western Missouri Mental Health Center Monday.

Mrs. White, Dianna's mother, understands that a lot of people come and go in big-city hospitals, that sometimes a patient is overlooked, perhaps even shunted away. But she doesn't think the medical treatment or the diagnosis her daughter received, which concluded that she was "just too fat" and "bizarre," was quite good enough.

"I thought it was a county hospital for everybody," she said Tuesday at her modest home in a white working-class neighborhood. "But I guess if you're rich it makes a difference. If only they had showed some concern and tried . . .

"If they had taken her into the room and taken her pulse or done anything but say it's all in her mind . . ."

Dr. Bonita Peterson, Jackson County Medical Examiner, is performing an autopsy to learn exactly what killed Dianna Bunyan.

The partly completed autopsy has not yielded that crucial information yet. But one thing has been learned: The 18-year-old woman was one and a half months pregnant.

Hank ''Bow Wow'' Arft

THE
SPORTING
LIFE

Play Ball!

It's not over yet

Every summer, it's the same thing. When a day's labor is complete, the not-so-young men shed their work clothes — their blue collars and their white collars — and pull on the colored jerseys that give them their stamp of distinction.

They play on a softball team. As predictable as the robin that pecks at the first buds of spring, they kick up dust on the infields of midsummer.

There's something pitiful about a man swinging a bat at a ball. Something in the way he grits his teeth so hard. Something in the way his aging muscles ache when he lurches in the wrong direction.

Something about the invisible spirit of youth that hovers over him, threatening to fly away.

But he thinks he's great. With his old leather glove, his jersey, his batting statistics, his fierce sense of competition. And he is great.

There he stands. Look at him. Somebody's husband. A breadwinner, maybe a father. A responsible man with a job. One foot on that ageless green bench, elbow resting on his thigh, his keen eyes survey the action on the field.

He tips his hat with his fingers. A baseball gesture. "All right," he shouts, "straighten one out. Make him pitch to you. Come on, now. Ducks on the pond!"

At home, his wife is putting the groceries away, planning dinner for her Babe Ruth. She gives the baby a bottle. "Daddy's playing softball," she says to the restless child.

There's the crack of the bat and it's Babe's turn at the plate.

"All right, get a hit. We need some runs," his teammates yell, a tone of terrible urgency in their voices. There is nothing else now, only runs batted in, only the white pentagon they call home plate, resting on the ground near Babe's feet.

He steps back from the plate and scans the outfield. He never scans the infield, because he plans to hit the long ball. The opposing outfielders are playing him in close, challenging him to hit it hard. They are challenging his manhood.

At home, the baby is crying now.

In his bones, Babe feels nervous. The strength in his arms gives way. He swings the bat nervously as the pitcher winds up. Here comes the pitch. The fat white ball, rising, spinning and falling, is coming to Babe. It is the object of his only desire.

His wife fills the bottle again. The baby is quiet.

Smack! A stinging line drive right at the pitcher's head. As Babe lurches toward first base, he watches the pitcher stumble and fall into the scorched dry dirt, evading the power of the Babe.

The shouts of his teammates urge him on. "Take two, Babe, keep goin'." He swings around first base, gritting his teeth, his flesh racked by a decade of beer and his eyes guided by the invisible spirit of his youth running just a step, now two, ahead.

The throw is coming in from the outfield to second base. The Babe heaves his overburdened body into the air, seeking forgiveness from God and the umpire, forgiveness from his wife and their unborn children, driven by the one unalterable principle of his life.

Passing through the air, while his wife and child wait together at the kitchen table, he catches the spirit of his youth. He joins with its richness and his life passes all at once through his bones. He will never be this great again.

He hits the dirt, bounces once, twice, his head ricocheting off the second baseman's shoe. The merciless tag. The second baseman, with the ball in his glove, raps the Babe's crumpled body in a defiant, triumphant tag out.

"Yer out," says the ump, with his thumb thrust up.

The Babe rolls over slowly, spitting the dirt from his mouth. The sky is blue and he can see it through the dust. His opponents are cheering but the Babe hears nothing.

A tattered jersey shrouds the aching body that lies motionless on the field. It is a pitiful failing of the flesh but it does not hide the greatness of the Babe.

He slowly rises and dusts himself off. It's just a twisted ankle, he tells himself, as the pain spirals up through his legs. He makes for the ageless green bench where he will sit for a while.

He can hear a teammate mutter, "No speed, no wheels at all." But it is the pain that draws his attention. Someone hands him his hat and he adjusts it on his head.

His fingers reach instinctively to tip the hat for the fans who didn't come, who didn't see the Babe lunge for all he was worth at the barred gate to second base.

At home, his wife checks the roast and tells the child, "Daddy's coming home soon now."

He limps home.

How'd it go, dear?

"We lost, but I hit a good ball in the last inning. Almost made it to second. Knocked the pitcher flat on his back."

The Babe trundles into the bedroom so his wife won't see the pain in his face. He sheds the torn jersey and sits on the bed, staring at nothing in particular.

Another game lost, he knows, but the summer is not over yet. The Babe's season is not over yet.

He
Works
the Series
for
Peanuts

Coca-Cola!
The words come hurtling through time, an echo from another age.
Leo Ernstein was just 20 years old on July 3, 1923, when the Kansas
City Blues opened their new ballpark at 22nd and Brooklyn.
Leo was selling Coke that day. Today he will be selling peanuts — 57
years, four ballparks and two home teams later.
Peanuts!
Leo Ernstein is a stout-hearted vendor. At 77 years old, he hustles a
living better suited to younger men. He shoulders his peanut rack,
ignores that touch of arthritis and treads the steps and stairs in search
of a fan who will answer his call.
"The fans are the nicest people in the world," says Leo, a man who
knows which side his bread is buttered on.
Leo belongs to the Yogi Berra school of philosophy. He won't dazzle
you with his wit or inspire you with his enthusiasm. He says things Yogi
might say, like, "I expected the World Series — as long as they were
winning ball games."
And like Yogi, Leo Ernstein came to play.
If not quite as strong as he once was, he is tough and determined to
"stay out of the rocking chair." Leo is tall and graying. His face is
accented by bushy, salt-and-pepper eyebrows, a toothless smile ("Thank
you, that'll be 50 cents") and long sideburns. He wears Adidas jogging
shoes and a Royals cap.
And for Leo Ernstein, this World Series in Kansas City is a dream
come true. He waited a long time to sell his first bag of World Series
peanuts.
Like most everybody else in the baseball business, Leo started in the
minors. His first day on the job in 1923, the Kansas City Blues defeated
the Milwaukee Home Brews, 10-7. At that time, Leo was selling just for

kicks. He loved sports and his job at Muehlebach Field gave him an opportunity to earn some extra money on the side.

By 1925, though, he got the itch to travel. A native Kansas Citian, Leo wanted to see more of the world.

"I traveled to Chicago," he remembers. "I was in Wrigley Field, Soldiers Field, Comiskey Park and then later I went on the road to Yankee Stadium."

In New York, he was selling soda pop while Babe Ruth was hitting home runs. He thought the Babe was "great" and remembers talking to him a few times.

In 1929, Leo was plying the stands of Wrigley Field when the Chicago cubs won the pennant behind the productive bat of Rogers Hornsby, who hit .380 that year. Leo was looking forward to his first World Series at the age of 26.

But illness in the family called him home to Kansas City. The Cubs went on to lose the Series — to the Philadelphia Athletics, a team that later moved to Kansas City.

Leo continued to work the stands through the '30s and '40s, but he admits he did it only sporadically. It wasn't until 1955, when Kansas City got its first major league franchise, that he started once again to peddle his wares every time the team played at home.

Twenty-five years of beer and peanuts later, the vendor finally finds himself in the World Series. It's a good feeling, he says. But don't get the idea that his mind is entirely on baseball.

When Game 4 is completed today, Leo will rest awhile and then hustle down to Kemper Area to sell peanuts at the Kings game. If the Chiefs weren't playing in Denver on Sunday, Leo would be at Arrowhead Stadium hustling nuts there, too.

In his career, he has played his game against a changing backdrop of basketball, rodeo, hockey, football, boxing and baseball. And after all those years and all that experience, what does Leo Ernstein have in the way of advice for the young vendors who follow in his tracks?

"I'm no schoolteacher," he says. "Let 'em find out for themselves."

In the competitive world of vending, only the fittest survive. That's Leo's message. A 77-year-old vendor, he must be pretty fit.

The single piece of advice Leo will give is this: "The fans are your lifeline. It's the people, the public . . . I like the fans because they're all good to me and they know me."

Today the vendor will do it again. The players will play their roles on the field. The fans will play theirs in the stands. And Leo Ernstein will sell his peanuts, battling time with a stout heart and a strong will. He simply will not relinquish his role.

"I do the best I can, for a vendor who's more than 77," he says. "And I hope I can come back next year."

Peanuts!

Bowling
is right up KC's
Alley

It has been said that bowling is one of Kansas City's favorite pastimes. No doubt this is true. Bowling alleys are in great abundance in the city, and more than a few locals have made a handsome living in the bowling shirt business.

Indeed some historians contend it was in the reign of King Louie that Kansas City recorded its happiest moments.

What does this say about Our Town? Do packed lanes bespeak a healthy preoccupation with physical fitness or the lack of anything better to do?

The issue is one that has haunted me ever since reading a Californian's published diatribe against Kansas City. High on the list of allegations directed against the city was the statement that bowling was highly regarded here. As a resident, I didn't know whether to feel insulted or complimented. Hence today's column, in which the appeal of bowling will be examined in some depth.

It should be stated at the outset that very few contemporary authors have attempted seriously to analyze the bowling question.

The reader's indulgence is therefore begged. If some aspect of the matter is neglected in this analysis, the reader should remember that bowling is a vast and complex subject area that cannot be comprehended in a few strokes of the pen. No doubt, other analysts soon will join in the study of this subject until it is laid utterly and finally bare.

With no more ado, then, the following is a preliminary inquiry into the appeal of bowling.

Numerous factors contribute to the popularity of the game, some of which leap readily to mind. There is, first, the spectacle of it all: the sounds, the smell of french fries at the grill, the thrill of the strike and the agony of the gutter ball.

And then there is the rented shoe. Here is an intangible in the sport of bowling and a possible factor in its appeal. In virtually no other activity does the participant have an opportunity to wear a rented shoe.

There is something about the rented shoe — which usually comes in a sporty two-tone color scheme — that seems to attract people to the game. Sometimes the shoe is still warm when rented, which is helpful if the bowler has circulation problems.

The rented shoe, however, does not compare in importance with the bowling shirt. The bowling shirt has been invested with enormous cultural significance. Bowlers are proud to be seen in their bowling shirts both on the alley and off. Bowling shirts, like antique furniture, increase in value with age.

Curiously, some of those same people who criticize the sport of bowling place a premium on the shirts. Although they would not be caught dead at an alley, they nevertheless may be seen scouring used-clothing stores for the prized bowling garb. They wear the bowling shirts to nightclubs and record shops, anywhere but to a bowling alley.

This bowling shirt data, although confusing, suggests that few remain indifferent to bowling and fewer still have never owned a bowling shirt.

One other accouterment of the game appears to contribute significantly to its appeal, and that is the bowling ball itself. The relative newcomer to bowling is reduced to using balls available on racks at the alley. But the veteran invariably will own his own ball.

The act of acquiring a bowling ball is a rite of passage. It represents the bowler's coming of age and is a statement of his commitment to the game. It is also a statement of his individuality. Bowling balls come in plain black (symbolic of macho violence), colored swirls (implying finesse), polka dots (for the feminine touch) and a host of other styles that seem to say: "I'm me."

In today's bowling world, the emphasis is on individuality. The modern bowler, perhaps feeling anonymous and unfulfilled at his or her job, purchases a charismatic ball and delivers it charismatically.

Some bowlers heave their payload, other release it smoothly. Some place a reverse twist on it, others keep it airborne until it is halfway down the alley. Whatever the technique, the bowler strives to make a unique personal statement before he retires to "The Ten-Pin Lounge" for a quick one.

Moreover, the bowler today is not satisfied to down ordinary white pins. He participates in specialty games called "Colorama," a variation of bowling in which the object is to strike down the colored pin and win cash. Cash, it appears, is of increasing importance in modern bowling.

Bowling, in conclusion, is a part of the great American tradition of rugged individualism. The sport thrives on flourish and highballs and collectible shirts. In diversity lies its appeal, and in rented shoes as well.

Get Along,

Urban Cowboy

This is the year the American Royal Livestock, Horse Show and Rodeo meets the Urban Cowboy.

The Royal, of course, has been around for years but the Urban Cowboy is a newcomer to the scene. He is the character who has made such a big splash lately in the fashion magazines. His jeans don't get dirty. His boots always are polished. He pays hundreds of dollars for his shirts.

The Urban Cowboy is, in short, the stylish city-dweller who has found that the Western Look is chic. Naturally he wants to go to the American Royal to bolster his image.

But the Urban Cowboy, for all his sartorial splendor, doesn't know a cow patty from a Big Mac.

He doesn't know which animal is which and is very likely to embarrass himself at the Royal.

That's why he needs this little tip sheet: The Urban Cowboy's Guide to the American Royal. This, Urban Cowboy, is for you:

The Cow: The cow is that large, short-haired creature you've seen eating grass in fields along the highway. If you rolled your window down you might have heard one shout "Mooo!"

You will impress your date if you explain to her that the cow is a female, too, and is responsible for the milk you drink and the Big Macs you eat.

The Bull is the male of the species who, unlike the **Steer,** is allowed by the farmer to go through life with his reproductive organs intact. A little advice: Go easy on the bull jokes. They're old hat.

Head is a term used commonly in the cattle world. The Urban Cowboy should try to remember that at the Royal, references to "head" have nothing to do with the lump of flesh he uses to hold up his 10-gallon hat.

Head refers to a single member of a herd — 14 head means 14 cattle, for example. The idea is that if you count the number of heads you'll have the correct number of cattle. It's much easier than counting hooves, especially if you are an Urban Cowboy and your hat is too big.

Heifer: Real cowboys use this word to talk about young cows that have not yet borne calves. Explain to your date that when you call her "my little heifer," as cowpokes sometimes call their wives and girl-friends, you are using a term of affection and not referring to her waistline.

That's all you need to know about cattle. Here's some key information about **Pigs, Hogs, Swine, Sows, Boars, Porkers** and other members of the **Bacon Family.**

These are the creatures with the rumpled snouts, the curled tails and the bad reputation. If the Urban Cowboy has ever watched Porky the Pig on television, he will know basically what to look for — except that real pigs don't stutter.

The bacon family offers the Urban Cowboy an opportunity to impress his date with some "inside knowledge" of the species. Pigs generally are considered to be slow, dirty and stupid. But this is not true. It's a bum rap.

The pig is quick, clean and among the smartest of all animals. If the Urban Cowboy should become confused at any time during the American Royal, he should seek out the nearest hog and ask for the necessary information.

Here are some quick tips on **Horses,** the most glamorous entries in the American Royal:

Remember when, as a child, you rode the merry-go-round? Well, the horse looks like that. Just add hair and a heartbeat. The **Mare** is the female; the **Stallion** is the male, intact: the **Gelding** is the male, no longer intact.

In addition to the jumping, cantering, trotting and walking for which horses are regarded so highly, horses have been known to exercise a strange effect on their often affluent owners. Some of the world's best-dressed people frequently can be found hunched over in a stall, preparing to haul the manure of their beloved horses.

The Urban Cowboy will want to avoid horse stalls and thereby leave the dirty work to real cowboys and society matrons.

There's only one more thing you need to know, Urban Cowboy: All about the **BOTAR.**

BOTARs (Belles of the American Royal) are not sold at market or led around the ring. The BOTARs are the young human females who are the hostesses of the Royal and the creme de la creme of metropolitan society.

They are lovely and elegant and their escorts are rather suburban-looking. BOTARs are cuter than heifers, smarter than hogs and more glamorous than horses.

Now be forewarned: Once you've gotten into the spirit of the Royal you may find yourself wanting to shout and hoot and stomp your feet. That's fine for the animals.

But, above all, remember this: Don't hoot or point at a BOTAR.

Or, Urban Cowboy, you may find yourself face down in a cow patty. You could muss up your Calvin Klein shirt that way.

The
Call
of the
Mud

She heard the call of the mud. Joanie Schadel wasn't sure where it came from exactly. Perhaps it was a whispering voice from some dark cavern in her subconscious. Or maybe it was a simian screech out of the distant evolutionary past.

When the call came — wherever it came from — Joanie went to the mud.

She wasn't the most likely candidate. A nice-looking middle-class woman of 29. The mother of a small boy. Nice job in the word-processing department at Farmland Industries, Inc. Former cellist with the Northland Symphony Orchestra. Ex-pompon girl at North Kansas City Senior High School.

Why would she want to wrestle in the mud with strong women while hundreds of barroom reptiles hiss, hoot, molt and drink beer at ringside?

It just goes to prove one thing about the call of the mud. You don't know where it will come from, or whom it will touch. It could touch you in the pit of the night, when you're angry and you don't know why.

For Joanie, it came not long after her boyfriend told her goodbye. He was moving to another town. She was angry with that fellow. Naturally, it came as quite a shock to him to learn by long-distance that she was now a mud wrestler.

For Joanie, it came at a time when that nice 9-to-5 word-processing job somehow wasn't adequately *fulfilling* for a former English major who graduated summa cum laude from Rockhurst College and liked to read Henry James.

For Joanie, the call of the mud came at a time when she just craved to do something fundamentally masculine, to be aggressive, to pare away emotions and just plain fight.

"People go to extremes when they're frustrated," she says, later adding something about the "need to be naughty."

Joanie remembers her first match a month ago at Hulio's Water Hole, a bar at Barry Road and North Oak: "It was kind of wild and noisy, with beer flowing everywhere. It was heady stuff, and I loved it.

It was the excitement of falling into the pen of mud and pinning the opponent and hearing the referee shout, 'One-two-three,' and winning.

"I remember sprawling across my opponent. To my horror, I discovered that I was pulling her hair. I was starting to apologize, when I had to catch myself and say, 'Joanie, be mean.'

"It was kind of elemental in there."

Being sufficiently mean required a little practice for Joanie. She was only 5 feet 4 and 110 pounds and not used to beating up people. She got her early training with "some real submissive" friends on the living room rug. So she wasn't ready when that first real opponent charged her, stuck a leg behind her and flopped her into the gaudy morass, mud flying into the crowd.

But Joanie wised up. She worked out with the young high school wrestler down the street. She concentrated hard and started to pretend that she was grappling with a "wrestling machine," not a person.

On Wednesday night, Joanie was back for her fourth encounter in the slime. Clad in a purple leotard, her stomach sucked in and her "best-build-in-the-graduating-class" body drawing guttural sounds from the reptiles at Hulio's Water Hole, Joanie pressed a persuasive case against a female bartender in a black leotard. For 20 minutes, they struggled in the mud.

For Joanie, it might have been some kind of grand purge, a venting of frustration or an assertion of power. For the mostly male audience, watching the women wrestle was a lustful experience. You could tell by the sounds they made as the struggle continued . . .

Twenty minutes is a long time in the mud. This is no quick-and-dirty exhibition. It is a battle. A winner must *endure* her opponent. If she does, she wins $50. If she loses, only $25. And Joanie was the victor. Her record, as she stumbled back to the dressing room, was 3 victories and 1 draw.

Being back in that dressing room, Joanie says, is like snaking down to view the underbelly of existence. The women eye each other warily, cut each other down when backs are turned.

"It's a little bit cutthroat," says Joanie. "It's an underside. I pretend I'm a reporter, or like I'm just gathering facts for a novel."

Joanie rejects the idea that mud wrestling is an exploitation of women. That never entered her mind, she says. No, rather than an exploitation of women, mud wrestling for her is a chance to break out of that office job, those stereotyped female roles, the ordinary mold of life.

Joanie heard the call of the mud. She heeded it. And, down there somewhere in the mire, she found satisfaction.

Rasslin'
fans are up in
Arms

The title bout was almost under way, and Nellie Kuehn was sitting in her regular seat decked out in an outfit that she dubbed "dressy western" — black slacks, a black-and-white striped jacket, a bright red blouse, and crystal beads and earrings.

Nellie, an attractive 58-year-old ex-waitress from Kansas City, Kansas, was screaming her lungs out.

"We want Bill! We want BILL! WE WANT BILL!" she shouted, louder and louder.

In the next seats over, Vern and Clara Beenblossom, some old friends who share the same section at Memorial Hall, joined the clamor, and pretty soon the huge auditorium was ringing with their cry. Down at ringside, another group picked it up: "We want Bill! We want Bill!"

Nellie was proud of this vocal spectacular, for it is Nellie who is behind the grass-roots bring-back-Bill-Kersten movement at the Thursday night All-Star Wrestling matches.

Kersten was, for 16 years, the impresario of Kansas City wrestling. He announced, interviewed the wrestlers and advertised the matches. All across the Midwest, television viewers recognized Kersten and his familiar "Hel-l-o-o, wrestling fans" invocation.

Bill was no Cary Grant, but to the fans, he was family. And that's why Nellie's so riled up. Kersten was fired in early December. His former boss, "Texas" Bob Geigel, explained then and still insists that the wrestling program "needed a change."

Well, Nellie and some other folks at the matches don't like the change. In the last two Thursday nights, Nellie has collected nearly 450 signatures of fans who say they want Bill Kersten back. About 2,000 attended the matches this past Thursday night.

One fan, Ray Minton, says that next week he's going to bring 4,000 bumper stickers to Memorial Hall. He wants to put the bring-back-Bill campaign on car bumpers across the metro area and says he's got some protest signs in the works, too.

Another change that Nellie's not to pleased with is Bill's replacement as ring announcer, Terry Garvin. An ex-wrestler himself, Garvin has been suited up in a tuxedo for his new job. Bob Geigel thinks it's classier that way.

But for some reason, the tuxedo really galls Nellie and other vocal fans at the matches.

"Bill Kersten has got personality," says Nellie, rattling her crystal beads. "That other guy doesn't speak to nobody. He don't know anybody — that stuffed shirt."

As Garvin begins to announce the title bout between world champ Harley Race and contender Bruiser Brody, some of the other fans direct similar remarks in Garvin's direction. Garvin appears not to notice and stands tall in his tuxedo, an incongruous master of ceremonies at an event that Fellini would relish.

"Sit down, ya stuffed toad," shouts one fan.

"We want Bill. Bring back Kersten," booms another.

"Get that monkey-on-a-stick outta the ring," demands one more.

Kersten, of course, is nowhere to be found. He has declined to attend the matches since losing his job. It wouldn't be right, he says. But Kersten is pleased that his fans would like to see him come back to replace the much-maligned Garvin.

"Wrestling fans are the most loyal type of fan there is," says Kersten. "They're proving it."

Terry Platt, one of those fans, illustrated Kersten's point when he said: "I grew up with Bill. Every Sunday on TV. Every Sunday. I work for BRB Construction, and I mean, what the hell, I grew up with Bill Kersten. He's the best thing that ever happened to rasslin'. They can't do this to him!"

And with that, the bout between Bruiser Brody and Harley Race got under way. The grass-roots campaign to bring back Bill subsided for a moment, and the real battle began.

As usual, there were crashing flips and bestial moans. There was strutting, and there was bleeding. There were small children looking on as gigantic men pummeled each other to the sweet music of the fans' exhortation.

When it was all over, the fans tramped through the blood on the floor at ringside, and some kids swabbed a bit of it up with their programs. The champion had won again.

The night was over for the wrestlers, for the stuffed toad in the monkey suit. And for Bill Kersten, it was another Thursday night away from Memorial Hall.

Nellie Kuehn vowed to return, though. She would bring more petitions; she would shout "We want Bill!" and she would berate Terry Garvin, "that yahoo."

Let's Win One for

Bow Wow

The talk, it seemed, all centered on Hank "Bow Wow" Arft.

I had never heard of Arft and neither had very many of my cohorts, but before long we found ourselves shouting things like "Let's win one for Bow Wow" and also things like "Bow Wow! Bow Wow!"

If a group of 15 grown men shouting "Bow Wow!" in unison strikes you as bizarre, then you may feel confident you have got the general picture.

It started simply enough as a reunion of college cronies who used to play softball on Cape Cod. I boarded the Boston-bound TWA jet with certain misgivings because reunions, it has always seemed to me, are too often marked by over-zealous backslapping and embarrassing pot bellies.

I arrived on the Cape expecting to join my team (known as the Boston Massacre) in a best-two-out-of-three-games softball contest against our longtime foes, the Low Tides. The teams had not met in battle since 1975. In spite of the air controllers strike, players journeyed to Cape Cod from such faraway places as Hollywood, Kansas City, Maine, New York City and Chicago.

Bow Wow Arft's letter was waiting for us when we arrived.

In his letter from the St. Louis suburb of Ballwin, Missouri, Arft expressed pleasure at being named the honorary chairman of the softball reunion. Writing on Schrader Funeral Home stationery, Bow Wow explained that since getting out of professional baseball, he had gone into the family funeral business, which had treated him well. He concluded by wishing us the best.

"Who," I asked, "is Bow Wow Arft?"

Will Scoggins, second baseman for the Boston Massacre, explained that Arft played first base for the St. Louis Browns in the late '40s and early '50s. Some months before the softball reunion, Scoggins and a few friends had been poring over a collection of baseball cards when one fell to the floor.

It was Hank "Bow Wow" Arft, of course. Lifetime batting average of .253. Born January 28, 1922, in Manchester, Missouri.

Apparently it was something about the nickname, something whimsical about Bow Wow Arft, the man, that had led to Bow Wow's selection as honorary game chairman.

With this explanation, Scoggins began to hand out Bow Wow Arft T-shirts commemorating the 1981 "Bow Wow Boogie" on Cape Cod.

At this juncture, the letter from Schrader Funeral Home and an autographed photo of Hank at the plate were examined carefully by various members of the Boston Massacre. Some members nodded their heads, others shook them in disbelief. Who was this Bow Wow Arft?

Later that evening, Scoggins reported that he had just received a phone call from Bow Wow in Ballwin. Bow Wow was very excited about tomorrow's game, Scoggins said. It was imperative that the Boston Massacre win one for Bow Wow.

This was inspirational, strange as it may seem. The mere possibility that a big-leaguer-turned-mortician was on our side aroused the group of aging softballers.

"Bow Wow!" we shouted.

The next day, it was "Bow Wow!" again as the Boston Massacre squared off against the Low Tides. With Arft rooting for us in Ballwin, we believed there was a lot on the line.

We won, of course.

Later, while a victory party (dubbed the "Bow Wow Cotillion") was under way, Will Scoggins announced that he had failed to contact Bow Wow with the good news. Arft was "with a family" and couldn't come to the phone.

The evening wore on and more unsuccessful phone calls were made. Some began to doubt this Bow Wow. Personally, I began to perceive Arft as a strictly mythical figure, created by Scoggins in an attempt to give a new twist to the reunion. Little more was said of Bow Wow after this, though the Bow Wow T-shirts were folded tenderly into suitcases when the weekend was over.

Back at my desk in Kansas City, I was haunted by this Arft. Was he real? I had memorized the funeral home telephone number and, unable to stop myself, I dialed it.

"Hank Arft," came the answer.

"Hank *'Bow Wow'* Arft?"

"Yes." Yes!

Bow Wow apologized for failing to contact the team on Saturday night after the game but, he said, he had been with a family. Arft once again expressed gratitude at being selected by strangers for his special role.

"I have a lot of calls and letters from people who want my autograph or some baseball shoes," said this man who played pro ball for $75 a month when he was just 18, "but this was the first time anybody wanted to have a softball game in my honor.

"I was truly honored."

NO BUSINESS BUSINESS LIKE SHOW BUSINESS

He's a
Rhinestone
Organist

"People don't think this is real," said Chris Skau, gesturing to his platinum hair and diamond jewelry. "They think I'm going to go home and take off the wig and rhinestone bracelets. They don't think Kansas City is the kind of place where people have these kinds of things. They think this is a redneck kind of place. But they're wrong. It's all real."

It is all real. The white shining hair is real, though bleached. The diamonds are real. So's the Lincoln Continental and the Yamaha computer organ that costs a small fortune. And indeed, so is Kansas City's own Liberace of the organ, 23-year-old Chris Skau.

Skau is determined to prove that a little bit of Vegas can get along in KC.

Most people know him as the Kansas City Royals' organist — the man behind the ballpark polkas, the "Take Me Out to the Ballgame" and the "Charge!" theme. But Chris Skau is more than that. He's show biz, year-round.

"The change in image came two years ago in June," Skau said, referring to his previously auburn hair and eyebrows to match (now the eyebrows don't match). "The hair change was a result of a lightening process I had done to it. One time it came out too light. Some of the people who knew me didn't like it too well, but others said, 'Oh, isn't that fantastic? Look at his hair — he looks like he stepped off a Vegas stage'."

He did look sort of Vegas a few weeks ago during an appearance at the Flower, Lawn and Garden Show on behalf of the Jenkins Music Co. One might not think organs would be a big entry at the lawn and garden show, but there they were, with Chris Skau playing them for all they were worth. Skau makes a lot of appearances for different organ companies, and this one was distinguished only by the fact that during his performance a woman jumped him and tried to pry one of the diamond rings from his hand.

But, as usual, Skau had his security man there — an off-duty Raytown police officer — and the ice stayed cool on his fingers.

For Skau, the hassle of being flashy is outweighed by the glamour of it all — and the money. He pointed out that if he stopped wearing the platinum hair, stopped wearing the $2,000 to $3,000 outfits for his nightclub show, took off the $100,000 to $200,000 worth of jewelry he wears, well, his value as an entertainer would decline.

Sure, Skau admitted he gets harassed by folks who might think he's a "cheap entertainer with bleached-blond hair," but he said, "It doesn't bother me, because we turn right around and laugh all the way to the bank."

These trips to the bank had their origin almost 24 years ago, when Ida Skau decided to play the piano in the mornings for her as-yet-unborn son. The morning lullabies may or may not have instilled musicality in the fetus, but by the time Chris was 4½ years old he was signed up to study at the Conservatory of Music, University of Missouri-Kansas City.

By the time he was 21, Skau had been performing for eight years professionally and had earned a doctor of organ performance degree from the American Association of Performing Artists. Now he sometimes refers to himself as Dr. Chris Skau.

The life of a teen-age organist wasn't always easy. Skau and his mother devised an elaborate security regimen for his performances at the Sir Loin Room downtown at the Phillips House hotel. After the performances, Skau would call his mother from a house phone and then scramble to his car at 12th and Wyandotte in the early morning hours. Arriving safely at his car, he would contact her by CB radio to say he was OK.

When Skau strikes up the organ for his sixth season with the Royals on April 13, he will have made sure that this year Kansas City fans know more about him. Skau was disappointed he didn't receive more publicity last year during the World Series.

"Here I play to 72 million people and we're getting letters from people all over the country about my music, but they don't know my name," lamented the organist.

So this year, Skau said, the Royals will flash his name on the score-board more and the organ booth will be open to the press during the games — a switch from the Royals' policy in the past.

And there's one more switch this year. Skau plans to appear after Royals games at Papio's, a restaurant and lounge at 8430 Prospect where Skau's company, CTS Enterprises, is building a 20-foot by 20-foot mirrored infinity room that will capture the magic of that computer organ, those diamonds and that platinum hair.

It'll be a little bit of Vegas for Skau fans who don't get enough at the stadium.

Talk back to
Jesus?
Ask Harry

It's business as usual for Dr. Jim Anderson and Harry Kinder, flying over Missouri farmland at 2,500 feet in a single-engine Beechcraft.

"Beautiful day, eh, Harry?" says Anderson. "Fine day to do the Lord's work." But he knows Harry won't have much to say.

The Beechcraft dips slightly, buffeted by convection currents, and Harry's wooden head bumps against the door of the aircraft. Harry, of course, feels no pain.

"We're going down now, Harry. Don't be nervous," Anderson says, chuckling to himself. Harry is non-plussed.

Anderson banks the plane into a final approach and skillfully guides it down into a cow pasture near the church. He stuffs Harry Kinder in a suitcase.

Striding toward the church, Anderson and Harry are ready to do their thing — a very unusual thing, as it happens.

You see, Anderson is the kind of preacher who speaks out of the side of his mouth. He's an evangelist-ventriloquist. Harry, of course, is a dummy.

The two have traveled tens of thousands of miles together, sometimes to tiny hamlets that offer Anderson's plane only a cow pasture for a welcome mat.

How does a 42-year-old Kansas City man end up flying around the Midwest with a dummy in tow, talking to people about Jesus Christ?

Glad you asked.

For Anderson it all began at the age of eight, when he saw his first ventriloquist performing at the Boys' Club here. Many years later, long after he resolved to enter the ministry, Anderson's fascination with the ventriloquist's art lingered.

He was a doctoral candidate at Southwestern Baptist Seminary in Fort Worth, Texas, when he met a ventriloquist who wanted to test a new teaching method. Anderson volunteered and before he knew it, he was speaking almost imperceptibly out of the side of his mouth.

The Big Break came in 1968 when he took his new-found talent to the greatest amateur show of all time, the Ted Mack Original Amateur Hour.

For the benefit of the television audience, Anderson recounted his entry into the Christian church. Then he introduced Harry Kinder, the dummy. Between the two of them, the act was a hit.

Anderson didn't win the amateur competition because, as he explains it, the show took place late in Ted Mack's career and the vote tabulation was never actually done.

But that didn't matter. In the coming days and weeks Anderson and Harry received telephone calls from people all over the country who wanted to book their act into churches and schools. They went on the road.

Before too long — after Anderson had graduated from the seminary and taken a teaching job at Springfield Baptist Bible College — the young evangelist-ventriloquist had another inspired idea. He would learn to fly.

Flying would enable him and Harry to travel quickly to engagements and would satisfy another new-found interest of Anderson's, missionary aviation.

Anderson had been touched by the story of five American missionaries who were killed in 1956 by primitive Auca Indians in the jungles of Ecuador. Among the five, Nathaniel Saint had shown great ingenuity as a pilot and, though he was killed, had paved the way for later missionary efforts.

But perilous journeys into South American backlands would have to wait. For the immediate future, Anderson decided to concentrate his aviation skills on getting him and Harry to the church on time.

In almost ten years, the evangelist-ventriloquist says, he's barnstormed all across Missouri and Kansas, with stops in neighboring states as well. And when this unusual team touches down, they go into their act.

The ventriloquism is mostly for the kids. Harry Kinder, the dummy, plays Everyboy, the kid who never goes to Sunday school, who lies and spits and gets confused.

While Harry and Anderson joke together, the preacher suggests alternatives to Harry's bad-boy behavior. The result is moral instruction delivered with humor. The kids "eat it up," says Anderson.

But the preacher's method does not end there. Inevitably Harry Kinder goes back into the suitcase and his boss takes to the pulpit with a more conventional brand of evangelism.

Columnist

is "super" in

Opera

It had been years since I'd sung in public, so you can imagine my surprise when the call came from the Lyric Opera.

I was flattered, sure.

"Mr. Brisbane," they said, "would you be good enough to appear in the Lyric's upcoming production of 'Fidelio'?"

I told them I wasn't sure if I'd be good enough, but I was certainly willing to lend my talents. It seemed like a heck of a deal.

The newspaper job had been getting to me lately and obviously was leading to a life of high anxiety and too much drink. Perhaps the artistic lifestyle would be more suitable to my sensitive temperament.

What was to be my role? I had never attempted opera previously, though I used to be a fairly good hand at Kingston Trio material. I was confident I could make the transition.

"You're going to be a flag bearer, Mr. Brisbane," they said. "Do you think you can handle it?"

A flag bearer. That sounded OK. I wasn't familiar with Beethoven's only opera "Fidelio," but I knew that old Ludwig, being a German, had a healthy appreciation for military pomp. A flag bearer in his opera would probably be a substantial part.

"You'll be a supernumerary," they said.

I wasn't at all sure what that was, but it sounded important. I decided to look up "supernumerary" in Webster's dictionary.

. . . that exceeds or is beyond the regular or prescribed number . . .

Perhaps I was to have an extraordinary role of some sort.

. . . extra . . . a person with a small, non-speaking part, as in a mob scene . . .

Oh. Uh, yes. I was beginning to get the picture. This was not a lead role, or even an extraordinary role. I was to be human theatrical fodder, a clod on stage.

I resolved to seize the opportunity anyway. You never know when the lead is going to come down with malaria, or something.

That was a couple of weeks ago. Now "Fidelio" has opened at the Lyric and will have its second performance Saturday night. In the interim I have learned quite a bit about the art and wile of the supernumerary.

If you are interested in this exotic creature of the theatre, come with me backstage where we supernumeraries are gathered before a performance . . .

It is 9 o'clock and the guys are dressing. The show started an hour and a half ago but we weren't in that part, so who cares? We can hear the opera in progress through a tinny speaker in one corner of the room.

We arrange ourselves with great care. When you're a supernumerary you don't get to speak or sing, so you place an awful lot of emphasis on your costume. Your self-respect is based entirely upon it.

You'll often see supernumeraries wandering through the corridors backstage, getting as much mileage as they can out of their costumes. Mine is dynamite — very militaristic, of blue and tan with nifty brass buttons.

Once the supernumeraries are dressed we hang around in the dressing room, recounting bigger roles in our career (I was Christopher Columbus in the seventh grade). Bob Snapp, a veteran "super" who plays a priest in "Fidelio," extends blessings to his cohorts while another super recites a few famous lines from other plays.

Suddenly, a trumpet blares through the speaker. A voice calls the entire cast to the wings of the stage and adds, in a footnote, "Supernumeraries, go to the corridor." Our moment has arrived. The final act begins.

Given a cue, I hoist my huge flag, about 12 feet of colorful carpet hung vertically on an aluminum pole, and proceed on stage.

I do so with a great sense of mission. As a supernumerary I know I have little opportunity to shine. It's not likely that anybody in the audience will say, "My, what a sturdy and talented flag bearer he is!"

However, (and here is the appeal of being a super) I do have ample opportunity to ruin the entire last act. One misstep and I could bring my giant banner down onto the heads of a large number of cast members. Or I could slip off the back of the stage, dragging the whole line of soldiers with me.

This would be a disaster. I know the director is counting on me not to do this. The knowledge gives me a sense of worth.

Fortunately, I succeed in marching erectly to my place on stage, where I stand immobile for about 15 minutes until the curtain falls. My job is to assume a military posture and hold it.

This is not easy, and when the audience applauds at the end I accept credit with a bow. The opera is over.

We supernumeraries congratulate each other. It's been another fine performance.

He was gonna be a
Star

Jimmy Holmes looks smart in his bell captain's uniform. Upright. Like a man who takes care of himself. Like a man who makes a point of doing his job right.

But Jimmy Holmes' eyes are tinged with sorrow, because he has led a life he regrets.

Twice every day he makes the trip to St. Mary's Hospital where his mother lies near death, unable to recognize him.

The 53-year-old bell captain bids her hello and tells her that he doesn't drink anymore. He tells her he's pulled himself together. But Jessie Stone, his widowed mother, just lies in her bed, crippled by strokes.

She stood by him when he was down-and-out, through all those years when Mr. Holmes' life was awash in booze. She defended him when friends said her son was a lost cause. Now the lost cause says he's found himself. And he wants his mother to know that her faith was not in vain.

But, it seems, it's too late for Mr. Holmes to make the point.

He is a slender man, of average height, with light brown hair neatly combed in a style that dates back to the days when Jimmy Holmes was going to be a star, or a hero, or better.

He was only 16 when he enlisted in the Navy and shipped out to fight World War II.

"I wanted to be a hero," he remembers. "That was what I had in mind. But they just gave me a mop."

Not much of note happened at sea, but while he was at liberty in New York City in 1942, Seaman Holmes encountered a man who would change his life — Louis De Rochemont, producer of newsreels and movies.

"He liked my looks," Mr. Holmes says. "And he said when I got out of the Navy to look him up in Hollywood."

So, like many other fortune-seekers in the post-war years, Jimmy Holmes went to Hollywood. He wanted to be a star. Louis De Rochemont made good on his word and put the teen-age veteran in four pictures.

They weren't very good pictures — "third-rate," Mr. Holmes says. The most successful was "Breakfast in Hollywood," which featured Jimmy Holmes in a minuscule role as a hitchhiking sailor.

Hollywood quickly turned sour for the aspiring actor. Every night there were parties and drinking. The established stars always appeared punctually on the set at 7 a.m. the next day, but not Mr. Holmes. He couldn't seem to handle the fast-track lifestyle of Hollywood.

Before long Mr. De Rochemont was advising Mr. Holmes to get out of town. He needed "stage experience," he was told. So he traveled back to Kansas City to make publicity appearances at theatres showing "Breakfast in Hollywood."

Mr. Holmes appeared on stage three times a day, introducing himself and telling audiences about the making of the film.

"Then I would attempt to sing, which I couldn't do," he says, smiling slightly. "They thought I ought to do something besides stand there."

By this time, Jimmy Holmes was an alcoholic. The end of the line in show biz was not far off. During the third show on a St. Joseph, Missouri, stage one day, he was so drunk he could barely stand up.

Fired by the theatre manager, he broke into the theatre office and took what he felt the manager owed him — $200.

The police found him in his room at the Jesse James Hotel, asleep in bed with the money next to him. The next day, Mr. Holmes says, the headline read something like, "Jimmy Holmes Makes a Personal Appearance on the Third Floor of County Jail."

What followed for the next 25 years in Downtown Kansas City were cycles of drunkenness and sobriety, employment and incarceration. The boy who wanted to be a hero cashed in his dreams for pints of liquor. His mother, who worked for many years at the Barrel Buffet, 12th Street and Central Street, looked on helplessly.

Mrs. Stone suffered her first stroke after she retired five years ago. Nursing homes and hospitals were in her future. Ironically, as his mother declined, Jimmy Holmes began to find new hope for himself. Alcohol, he discovered, was poisoning him. Slowly, and not altogether totally, he quit it.

He was hired as a bellboy at the Phillips House hotel. Then, when it closed down, he worked at the Dixon Inn where they made him bell captain. The Phillips House re-opened in May of this year, and Mr. Holmes was hired back as bell captain there, with seven bellboys working under him.

He does a good job there. But there is much regret about the past.

"What I want is for people to know that after all these years my mother didn't waste her time raising a drunk," he says, a frustrated and remorseful man.

The Indian
Rubber
Girl earns no
Salary

Why did I go to the freak show?

That is the question I find myself grappling with after a visit to the Missouri State Fair at Sedalia. There were plenty of other attractions to catch the eye.

In fact, the State Fair proved to be an impressively sprawling, big account of human affairs. It was a mirror on Midwestern society, packed into corrals and brick exposition buildings along the midway and Swine Boulevard, on the track and in the barns and stables, even in the Coon Dog Water Pit and corn dog stands.

In the home economics building, I saw the delicate handiwork of Missouri quilt-makers who have added new dimensions to an old art. I saw an older woman who stared at one fine quilt and declared to her friend, "I'd go cross-eyed doing that."

I saw short, purple "novelty corn" with a blue ribbon on it. There were monstrous trios of pumpkins, too, and watermelons of gigantic girth.

I saw a horse show, conducted in the hot coliseum where electric fans blew damp air across a slow ritual of equine elegance. "Hold him tighter, keep his head up," said the woman in the stands as her friend cantered by on the rail.

I saw 6-year-old Brian, lead singer in his family's country music band. With a paper cook's hat on his head, he sang "Rollin' in My Sweet Baby's Arms" in a wobbly soprano. And as the family quintet broke into "Rocky Top Tennessee," the Pleasant Hope High School Band marched by the tent blaring out a competing wave of music. It was a dreamlike cacophony of pure Americana.

So why did I go to the freak show?

I saw native art in the fine arts building. Artists' hands had recreated the simplicity of nature and the complexity of human emotion. I looked on as a woman gazed in delight at "Herman and His Big Fish," an enormous painting of a blue-eyed old man and the ultimate catfish.

I listened in as Junior's mother told the boy, "Well, Junior, I guess you're just not a big enough boy to go to the State Fair." Junior held his head in his hands, humbled by his mother's judgment, crying at the table. Maybe he wasn't a big enough boy to go to the State Fair.

I saw a fat man at a fried chicken tent, who said, "I heard of people starved to death because they were too lazy to feed themselves."

And I saw the sardonic Bobo at the Dump Bobo In The Water game, who shouted to a young girl, "Hey, Blondie, is it true blondes have more fun? So what are you doin' with that guy?"

So why did I go to the freak show?

Inside the freak show, the quilted tapestry of the State Fair gave way to the loose ends, the knots and mistakes of creation. There were no blue ribbons in the freak show.

The Alligator Man explained to a gawking, timid audience that "I've been this way since I was 4½." Small patches of rough, darkened skin gave him his name and the freak show gives him his livelihood.

The Monkey Girl, bearded and hairier than most men, told us, "I'm the only one in my family born this way. Why, only God knows." She said she was married and had children. Her son is a Marine.

Popeye stared at the crowd, dressed in powder blue slacks and a frilled shirt, and said, "Keep one eye on the lef' eye, one eye on the right eye and one eye on Popeye!" And then his eyeballs pushed slowly forward from their sockets until he looked like a bug-eyed alien in a science-fiction movie.

Inside the freak show, a barker announced each act, one after another. Sometimes he called for more money from the audience. "The Indian rubber girl earns no salary so, please, a quarter from each!" he would say.

And with each succeeding act, I felt a cycle of emotions. First, it was curiosity stemming from the barker's description. Next it was fear of the unknown and grotesque. When the freak was finally unveiled, though, I felt a sense of familiarity because no matter how strange the person appeared, his humanity showed through. The freak show promises freaks but delivers people who remind us, perversely, of ourselves.

And finally, I felt degradation. The perversion was not simply in the genes of the freaks, but in the genes of the audience. We shared it, those of us who were inside the freak show.

Back out on the midway, 6-year-old Brian was singing "Rollin' in My Sweet Baby's Arms" again and I was wondering, "Why did I go to the freak show?"

It's the
Swingingest
lobby in
Town

It's a funny thing when the people you meet are surprised you're still alive.

"Dott, is that you, Dott?" they say. To which you answer, "Yes, it's me. Who else?"

Indeed, who else but Dott Bossi Jackson, KC's 76-year-old keyboard queen who started on piano in a silent-movie house in Humansville, Missouri, back around the end of the First World War?

It couldn't be anybody else but this vivacious downtowner who has lived in Kansas City hotels for the last 30 years.

You're not likely to confuse her with any other septuagenarian organists still pounding out melodies in this town. Mrs. Jackson has a personality you can't overlook and was once billed as "the friendliest entertainer in Kansas City."

Now, of course, most of her old haunts are really haunted. They're dead and gone. History.

As she says, "It's pitiful when you outlive all the buildings."

These days Mrs. Jackson can be found playing the organ in the lobby of the Dixon Inn hotel, Downtown at 12th Street and Baltimore Avenue. It's a jaunty scene there, 11:30 a.m. to 1:30 p.m., as she plays tunes from her catalog of 2,000 or so of the greatest hits since Scott Joplin.

A recent weekday at the Dixon Inn lobby found Mrs. Jackson seated behind the organ dressed in a smart skirt and blouse with a white vest. A couple of guys were sitting in the lobby reading the paper and tapping their feet.

A man, checking into the hotel about 1 p.m., stood at the desk wearing a jacket that said, "Chuck's Welding and Repair." He looked rather surprised as Mrs. Jackson, seizing the moment, broke into "You Must Have Been a Beautiful Baby."

The whole idea of the organ in the lobby, you see, is to welcome the guests with a little musical message, to create a livable lobby. The desk clerk, Bud Talbert, appreciates it. And so do the guests.

A gentleman from India showed up the other day and the organist segued right into "Oh, Calcutta." A Texan appeared and it was "San Antonio Rose."

Most people don't expect to find an organist in the lobby. It creates a soap-opera effect, and people like the heightened drama.

Of course, Dott Jackson will admit that playing a lobby isn't quite as glamorous as playing the Drum Room at the Hotel President, or the Alley Room at the Pickwick Hotel, or the Zebra Room at the Aladdin Hotel, or even the Glass Hat in Joplin, Missouri.

Those were some of Mrs. Jackson's old venues. They're all history now, as is the era in Kansas City when organists could be heard at a multitude of hotel bars and lounges.

Those were the days when the well-heeled left big tips for requested songs, when people left cabs waiting at the curb, when Mrs. Jackson had a host of contemporaries who vied for pre-eminence in the organ game.

The competitors are all dead now.

But Mrs. Jackson doesn't let it get her down. Music buoys her. "There's something sacred about it," she says. "Music is religion to me."

She recalls the many times that a favorite song has won smiles and the times a song brought a tear. She remembers the mysterious Marie Gargotta, widow of slain gangster Charles Gargotta. Marie used to ride taxis late into the night and regularly dropped by Gus' restaurant and lounge, 1106 Baltimore Ave., where Mrs. Jackson was playing in the '50s. Gus' is a parking lot now.

The widow would leave the cab waiting at the curb and, running into the lounge, would ask the organist to play, "Charlie, My Boy" one more time. Marie made this a regular practice until August 17, 1961, the night she died of natural causes in the back seat of a cab.

Now, of course, Downtown Kansas City isn't the entertainment district it used to be. And anyway, as Mrs. Jackson points out: "There's not that much demand for a 76-year-old playing organ. Let's face it."

Still, the organist is content to crank out the familiar melodies in the lobby and continue living Downtown.

"It's a way of life with me," she says, relaxing in her sixth-floor room at the Dixon Inn, where memorabilia fill the walls and shelves. "Living Downtown is like living in a little town. It's like a little neighborhood. I walk down the street, I know most of the people I meet . . .

"If you want to be with people you go down to the lobby. If you want to be alone you put up the 'Do Not Disturb' sign."

Initiated into show biz in tiny Humansville, Dott Bossi Jackson is determined to finish her engagement right here in Kansas City. You can catch her act in the lobby.

He/she
has the Jewel Box
Blues

When Ray Rondell got the news a week ago, he was crushed.

He would be out of work after Saturday night, just another statistic in an era of hard times. He was angry, and he was depressed.

His prospects were not good. Naturally, he would file for unemployment compensation. But he knew that finding work in his chosen profession would be almost impossible in Kansas City. The job market for female impersonators is very soft.

It was a lousy break, but whoever said female impersonation was such a promising field to begin with? Ray Rondell had barely scraped by on his earnings. He harbored no illusions about becoming a world-famous female impersonator. He had gotten used to the late hours and abusive audiences, the creeps who paid money to harass the performers.

So it was almost cruel what happened on Saturday night, the night of Mr. Rondell's last engagement. Instead of the usual paltry crowd at the Jewel Box, hundreds of Kansas Citians turned out to witness the last hurrah of this, Kansas City's only female-impersonation bar.

The smoke was thick inside, and a line formed outside. There were preppies and pimps and retired impersonators on hand. The transsexual community was well-represented. The audience, so diverse, responded as one — with enthusiasm.

The excitement in the dressing area backstage was palpable. Interviews were conducted, guests dropped by, a fellow impersonator from California paid a courtesy visit and asked to borrow a gown. A guest appearance was in order. After all, this was a momentous occasion.

Backstage, the performers could hear the invigorating sounds of people clapping, not teasing. This was the nearest thing to real show business witnessed at 31st and Main streets in a long time.

This was glamour, or at least a reasonable facsimile of it to go along with the exotic costumes and the wigs and the sequins that were soon to be packed away.

So where were all these people when the Jewel Box really needed them? Ray Rondell had to wonder. He shook his head slowly and grinned. If only they had come before . . .

A 32-year-old man in a wig and dress, he said, "All my life I've been a day late and a dollar short."

He certainly missed the heyday of the Jewel Box. The club has offered female impersonation for more than 20 years and in earlier years used to pack in large crowds. But the exotic art apparently lost its attraction somewhere along the line. Few have dared recently to venture into a neighborhood where the lights burn late in a pornographic bookstore, a strip joint and a female impersonation bar.

Middle-class patrons, who once went to the Jewel Box to satisfy their curiosity or to play voyeur for an evening, wrote the place off. Their fantasies were not worth the risk anymore.

The entertainers continued to perform, of course. They were professionals who took pride in the knowledge that the Jewel Box had a national reputation. But the glamour was fading and the photos of Ray Rondell, Sandy Kay and the other attractions were, too.

It was almost cruel, this brief reprise of a declining art. What would happen now to Ray Rondell, Sandy Kay, Renee Scott and Arcadia Lake? What happens to female impersonators who reach the end of the line?

Ray Rondell, for one, won't give up. "I'm going to use any vehicle I can," he said. "But I'm going to keep going."

Arcadia Lake, who physically resembles a woman, plans now to perform as a female stripper. No one will notice the difference.

Sandy Kay and Renee Scott won't abandon show business either and cling to hopes of taking their act on the road.

But none will return to the little nightclub at 31st and Main streets. The wrecking ball will claim the Jewel Box. And when it does, it will claim, too, a curious niche of society, a place where men dress as women and where once people paid to see it.

It was a vigorous last hurrah, though, wasn't it? Sandy Kay was Judy Garland one more time. Renee Scott was Diana Ross. The audience brought money, and they drank every Budweiser in the house.

For an evening, the Jewel Box remembered the good old days. Then the Jewel Box died.

Ray Rondell was unemployed.

Politics
is good
Theater
in Westport

Tombo Burke mounted the soapbox with a sense of urgency in his heart and gin in his belly. For an instant, and only that, the sloshing sounds at the bar ceased. Tombo's opponent — the gargantuan Fuzzy Perkins — stood by, sullen, kneading his overcoat with nervous hands.

It was the beginning of the political season in Westport, an eating and drinking district that is not a municipality but a state of mind, of inebriation.

Each year the Westport crowd elects a mayor not so much for representative government but just for the hell of it. The position grows more prestigious with time. Tombo Burke and Fuzzy Perkins both very much want to be mayor. You can hear it in their words, smell it on their breath.

There Tombo stood, the picture of an iron-backed, hard-living Irishman. He wore a black derby on his head. A white beard curled around his jaw from temple to temple. At 52, Tombo has sailed the high seas, fashioned boilers, tended bar and told several off-color jokes.

"I'm the only candidate who actually works in Westport," he shouted to the rude gathering at Elephant Johnnie's.

Elephant Johnnie's, a new watering hole in the district, made a perfect setting for this bloated political event. Formerly called the Red Head Lounge, Johnnie's is a fairly small establishment built around a circular bar. On the walls are tall mirrors, which create a multifaceted view of the goings-on around the bar.

It's the perfect place for politicians and other hustlers. While talking to one person, a pol can be looking at six others and, with practiced use of the mirrors, can even see what's going on behind his head.

When Fuzzy Perkins is in the room, you can see him everywhere. Perkins, a 34-year-old pilot who weighs "in excess of 350 pounds," is a former mayor of Westport who wants to get his hands on the throttle of power again.

He and Tombo Burke were locked, on this occasion, in a preliminary skirmish — a caucus. Each made speeches and then spoke with the press. Two candidates — Pam Britton and Maureen Thiede — had failed to show up, a move that left pundits wondering whether the two women candidates could hope for a chance in the general election on Monday.

Launched on the soapbox, Fuzzy Perkins cut quite a figure. His girth was wrapped in a natty tweed jacket that opened to a size 30 shirt collar. His animated head was topped with Fuzzy's most endearing physical trait: tiny, disparate tufts of light-colored hair.

He spoke with the air of a man who wants his office back.

"I'm down in Westport night after night, guzzling drinks," he boomed to the liquid set, "representing you . . .

"My opponents have a lot of guts running against the only guy who should be mayor — ME!"

Of course, both candidates promised the world. Tombo promised better looking women from Kansas. Fuzzy promised "to eliminate crime in the street totally by widening the sidewalks." Both promised more graft and corruption.

But, as in any political campaign, there's more to winning than shouting the right promises from a soapbox. You have to buy the right people.

To handle the press, Fuzzy has hired political consultant Jerry Jette, who admits he signed on for $2.98 but insists, "I rarely sell out for less than $3.98."

Despite the consulting expertise of Jette, it appeared Perkins might have made a major political gaffe Thursday night at the caucus. While discussing his background he let slip the fact that he once lived in Cleveland.

The crowd near Fuzzy shrank back in horror. "Cleveland?" they wanted to know.

Fuzzy did some fancy stepping and pronounced: "Yeah, but I wasn't born there. There's a sign over the place I lived. It's a shrine in Cleveland."

Only time will tell, as the pundits like to say, but Fuzzy's Cleveland gaffe may prove to be political dynamite.

Adding to Fuzzy's troubles, Tombo Burke quickly unveiled his own revolutionary plan for Westport. He mumbled something about holding a "charitable ball" there to raise funds for an unspecified needy cause. Emerging as a Reform Candidate, Tombo appeared to be appealing to the electorate's sense of altruism, never before a factor in the Westport mayor's race.

"It's been (deleted) around here for three years," he blurted out. "I think it's got to take some direction, seriously speaking."

Will Fuzzy Perkins find happiness in the mayor's office again? Can Tombo Burke bring charity and graft together in a happy political compromise?

The election Monday will tell all.

CAFE
KANSAS
CITY

The
President
drops in for a
Bite

Ed. Note: Lightfingers Louie, a bagman on his monthly run from Brooklyn to KC, was on hand at the historic meeting between the president and Arthur Bryant Monday and honored us with this account:

A little boidie tol' me the president was comin' to Bryant's Barbecue, so I wen' down there to get some lunch.

Ordinarily, I don' fool with lunch much and prefer to drink it, ya know? But dis was different, so I decided to have a ham-beef combo. Easy on the fries, Mr. Bryant, I ain't young anymore.

I get down there about 12-toity and the line is this long. So what else is new? Everybody likes to eat dat junk, so I figure I'll take my time. The little boidie who tol' me about President Carter said he would be arrivin' at 2.

You might be wonderin', don't I got somethin' better to do than go down to some barbecue joint and wait for the president? The answer would be dat, yeah, usually I got better things to do, but not on dis particulah day. So shut up and let me tell the story.

Foist thing I noticed was this guy who comes in with a wire stickin' outta his ear. Now, you can always tell a fed by dat wire dat's stickin' out of his ear. Dat's how they talk to each other.

Mr. Bryant was over at the back — he wasn't lookin' too spiffy, considerin' the president of the country was gonna be there — and he was talking to a repairman from Re-Nu-A-Light, Inc. (I read it off his shoit) and then he was talkin' to the fed.

So I'm sittin' there with my ham-beef combo and the next thing ya know, there's a photoger . . . a photoguf . . . there's a guy with a camera outside on the sidewalk and some more feds walkin' aroun.

This fat guy at the front table noticed some commotion and leaned back to check it out (he had his back to the door, somethin' I would never do) and when he leaned back, he bumped up the table with his fat belly. I got a laugh outta dat one, I'll tell ya.

At dis point, I figure I'm the only guy, except Mr. Bryant, who knows dat the president is going to eat barbecue here, and I'm laughing at the fat guy as he gets up to leave. I mus' admit I was pretty disappointed when I hear dis pretty little goil, about 9 years old, say,

'I'm waiting for the president.'

Sheesh, I thought I had the inside dope.

A couple minutes later things really start to hop. Ya can see cops out on the sidewalk and more feds are comin' in the door.

I mus' admit I'm a little nervous at dis point, on account of a little jam I got into back in New York in '67. But these feds are too young to remember me.

These feds are sharp. They got little insignias on their lapels. Their hair is all in place.

Ya know, you can always tell a fed. I can smell 'em. But even ordinary people can tell feds. You remember those 'dry look' commercials? Dat's what a fed looks like.

By dis time, there are feds at the Coke machine, feds at the counter, feds at the back room, feds on the sidewalk, cops on the street and dat little goil is sayin', 'I'm waiting for the president.'

But you'd be surprised how dumb people are. Some of 'em are jes' sittin' there with their beef and gettin' sauce all over their faces. They don't know what's up. Could be Mussolini pullin' in for all they know. Sheesh. Guys with red stuff in their mustache. Me, I'm done by now and just polishin' off this jug a beer.

All of a sudden, dis big fed wit' blond hair (I don't miss much) stands up and shouts — while all these people are tryin' to eat lunch, unnerstan' — 'The president is comin' for lunch. Anybody wants to stay, he can stay. Anybody wants to leave, they can leave now.' He made 'now' sound like Right Now.

I got the shakes. Ya know, kinda like ya just got outta the joint and you're afraid of cars in the street. I just got nervous.

'If you're stayin', we need to do a little search on ya.'

Sheesh. They wanted to search me. I start easin' on out of the picture, ya know. The big guy with the blond hair — I'm startin' to remember how much I hate feds — he's friskin' the guys with sauce in their mustache. A blond chick is friskin' the women. Arthur Bryant is runnin' around in the back. I couldn't really see what dat guy was up ta.

I looked out the window and thought I saw the president, but it was only Wendall Anschutz. I better get outta here.

I was just about out the door when I got blown down by a stampede of guys with cameras and guys with wires comin' outta their ears. There musta been a hundred of 'em.

I'm hidin under a table and in comes the president and his wife. He's a real little guy. They set him down with a plate o' beef and fries, and her, too. He doesn't have a mustache, but he did get dat red sauce on his face. Mr. Bryant was smilin' next to Carter, although I think he liked Truman better.

I fel' sorry for Carter. Here's dis nice guy wit' his wife and they're tryin' to eat barbecue with cameras stuck in their plates and everybody is writin' down dat he got sauce on his face. What if the Russians read dat?

I overheard Mr. Bryant say, 'If I'd a known you were comin,' I woulda baked a cake.'

Lemme outta here.

One
Whopperburger,
To Go

WHOPPERBURGER, INC.,
a Kansas corporation
vs.
BURGER KING CORP.,
a Florida corporation

The trial of the century? No, but it's one whopper of a mess anyway.

It seems that these two corporations waged a titanic battle over the use of the word "whopper," and now that the smoke has cleared, a fellow named Terry Blaylock is feeling pretty well-grilled. It's a complicated story, this tale of two whoppers, so let's take it from the top.

The Kansas whopper came first, after Vernon F. Barrow established the Whopperburger restaurant at the corner of Johnson Drive and Beverly Street in 1953. The sign there became a landmark, hulking over a road that once was dirt and now is a busy suburban thoroughfare.

Pretty soon the Whopperburger sign is going to have to come down, though. Mission, Ks., is losing its claim as the true home of the whopper.

The Burger King Corp. first began calling its burger the "Whopper" back in 1958. In 1965 the Whopper trademark was certified by the U.S. Patent Office. After that, the franchise corporation held claim over the whole lingual kingdom of Whopperdom. Nobody could call anything a Whopper and sell it, except the boys at Burger King.

For years the two homes of the Whopper coexisted peacefully. This, in all likelihood, was because Burger King was not aware of its whopping competitor in Kansas.

Mr. Barrow's successor, Lou Bernstein, bought the Whopperburger stand in the mid-'50s and sometime later — it's not clear exactly when — he got a few letters from the Burger King attorneys.

"They tried to get me to stop using the name," Mr. Bernstein said. "BUT I HAD IT FIRST!"

The feisty Mr. Bernstein would not be whipped and continued to sell Whopperburgers, undaunted. His successor, however, was not so fortunate. After Ronald L. Gold bought the Whopperburger restaurant in 1978, Burger King asked him to drop the "Whopper" in

122

Whopperburger. But Mr. Gold, being an attorney, decided to sue Burger King before it could sue him.

He won, sort of.

The federal court ruling, issued in March 1979, ordered Mr. Gold to quit using " 'Whopperburger,' or any other name or mark confusingly similar to (Burger King's) registered marks 'Whopper' and/or 'Home of the Whopper,' except that this injunction shall not apply . . . in connection with the existing Whopperburger . . . "

In other words, Mr. Gold could not use "Whopper" except where he already was using it. The court ruling also required that if the restaurant were sold, the new owner could no longer use "Whopper."

Enter Terry Blaylock, a 31-year-old father of three and a businessman. He bought the restaurant from a bank, which had foreclosed on Whopperburger. The little stand apparently had fallen on hard times under the ownership of Mr. Gold's successor, Paul Cinnamon.

When Terry Blaylock took ownership, he didn't know about the previous lawsuit between Burger King and Mr. Gold. He blithely continued to call the place Whopperburger.

Then, on December 26 of last year, I wrote a column about Mr. Blaylock's Whopperburger stand, calling it "perhaps the most historic hamburger stand in Johnson County." Within weeks after the publication of that column, two things happened:

First, Ronald Gold contacted Mr. Blaylock, and claiming ownership rights to the name "Whopperburger," demanded that Mr. Blaylock drop the name or else pay him $50 a month to use it.

Second, the Burger King Corp. contacted Mr. Blaylock, also claiming ownership rights, and simply demanded that Mr. Blaylock quit using "Whopperburger" altogether.

Terry Blaylock was getting it from two sides — a sandwich play, if you will. He was willing to fight Mr. Gold, but with the court ruling clearly in favor of Burger King, he opted to give in to Burger King.

He isn't happy about it at all. Mr. Blaylock seriously doubts that anyone would confuse his stand with a Burger King.

"We don't have people come in and go, 'Oh, I thought this was Burger King,' " he said. "They know where they're at. They know what they're eating. So what's the big deal? I really do have a little regret that I'm not big enough to take these guys on."

So, alas, within three weeks all traces of "Whopper" will have been banished. Mr. Blaylock plans to hold a contest to come up with a new name. In the meantime, he can't even answer the phone, "Whopperburger of Mission."

It's a hamburger tragedy.

His
Shakes
still live in
Memory

The king of the milkshake is dead. Roy Herndon passed away over the weekend and, for those who once tasted his miracle concoctions, the obituary notice brought back memories of the days when milkshakes were milkshakes and malts were malts.

For nearly 50 years, Roy Herndon was a fixture at Robinson's Drug Store, first at 12th and Brooklyn and later at 34th and Main. Roy worked the counter for most of his career. A handsome black man who wore a starched collar and tie even as he plied the fountain, Herndon lived for his work and some days worked 17 hours for his living.

Mary Tidona, who owns Jimmy & Mary's Steak House across the street from the old soda fountain and pharmacy, remarked upon hearing of Roy's death: "He made the best milkshakes in Kansas City. People used to come from all over. We were pretty busy over here, but I'd find time to go over for one of his milkshakes. They don't make them like they used to."

No, they don't. Time has corrupted the art of the soda fountain. These days fast food chains serve an unidentifiable milky sludge and call it "milkshake."

Time has made history of Robinson's Drug Store, too. By 1959, the store was closed and Roy Herndon had embarked on his retirement years. Now a pornographic bookstore has replaced the old soda fountain at 3325 Main.

And, finally, time made history of Roy Herndon. Living into his 87th year, Roy was taken from his home at 2402 Olive on Saturday night. He died the next day at the hospital.

Inside the old house, his widow, Helen, remembered Roy's beginnings with Samuel Robinson — who was a "good man," she says. Roy was a 17-year-old delivery boy for Robinson when he and Helen started dating. After the Herndons were married, Robinson moved the store to Main Street and it seemed to the Herndons that everybody who was on the way up in those days was headed south.

So Roy and Helen headed south, too, from their place at 18th and Brooklyn. With some financial help from Robinson they bought their house at 2402 Olive and settled in for a lifetime. It was in that house that Helen cooked the roast beef that was to help make Robinson's such a popular lunch and dinner spot.

As Walt Bodine, radio and television personality and former patron of Robinson's, remembers it: "Roy had a beef sandwich that was the tenderest, tastiest beef I've ever eaten. I've never to this day figured out how he cooked it. He'd bring it out already cooked. You could just sit there and eat beef sandwiches until you were ashamed of yourself. And then you'd eat two more."

It was Helen who cooked that beef, but the secret of its seasoning is lost to time and her fading memory.

What remains vivid, though, is the image of Roy behind the counter. A somewhat formal man who made a point of joining social clubs, Herndon was never seen without his collar and tie. He gloried in his reputation and the high-class clientele who frequented Robinson's.

J.K. Russell, a retired schoolteacher who was Herndon's friend, recollects: "He had nothing but that drugstore in his heart. That's all he talked about was Robinson's Drug store. That was what his name was tied up with.

"He always was bragging about the top people who came there from up on Armour Boulevard back in those days."

When they'd come from Armour — or from the business district in Midtown — they'd see a long counter with places for 10 or 12 people. They'd see round, marble-topped tables. And frequently they'd see crowds filling all the seats. Roy would be exchanging pleasantries with the regulars.

Bodine, whose father was a druggist, recalls the smells of Robinson's Drug Store. They were pharmaceutical smells, of substances ground by mortar and pestle. "And hovering over the smell of different things mixing," he says, "was the maddening smell of Roy's beef."

Those were the days when drug stores still smelled of drugs. When countermen knew the difference between a milkshake and a malt. When you were served an entire shaker of milkshake, not an 8-ounce glass. Those were the days when milkshakes were milkshakes and malts were malts.

"I remember the day I went over there, mouth watering for Roy's beef and one of his malts, and there was a sign that said they'd closed down," says Bodine. "That was the moment that marked the decline of the republic."

Twenty years later the king of the milkshake has gone to his reward. He leaves behind a wife and a lot of customers who remember when. . .

125

With a Mac,
The
attack
comes free

Persons of the tropical persuasion have a much more sensible approach to the working day. After a leisurely lunch, they retreat for a siesta of several hours' duration. Suitably rested, they return to their endeavors.

We in America, however, prefer the American way of lunch. It's part of our much-ballyhooed "work ethic." It's also gastrointestinal disaster.

For a close-up look at this tradition we call the lunch break, let's trundle over to City Center Square with The Luncher. The Luncher is only trying to find nourishment, quickly, but in the heart of the downtown scramble for life, liberty and the pursuit of a paycheck, he finds more. Or is it less?

Standing in the middle of the indoor plaza at City Center Square, The Luncher is faced with a choice of quick eats. He is also caught up in some major pedestrian traffic as hundreds, perhaps thousands, of Kansas Citians press on toward the gleaming lunch counters.

The Luncher selects McDonald's, agreeing with the slogan that says, "You deserve a break today." Indeed he does deserve it, but he doesn't get it at McDonald's.

The Luncher is pinioned between hustling lunchers who have queued up in half a dozen lines while frenzied counterpersons take orders and deliver neatly wrapped packages of McDonald's food. The Luncher is deciding upon a McChicken with large fries and a medium Coke when in the middle of his unsteady contemplation of food, a counterperson starts blowing a McDonald's whistle. This indicates that somebody has won something, but The Luncher does not immediately grasp the meaning of it all.

"Large-Coke-fries-Big-Mac-here-you-go-thank-you-Hi-may-I-help-you?" says the counterperson, dispensing with one luncher and addressing The Luncher, who places his order and receives it in something under 35 seconds.

The Luncher, his booty in a bag, begins his hunt for a table. Inside the McDonald's in City Center Square there is an official McDonald's seating area, but it is divided by strange mirrored walls and, because of the mass of lunchers therein, the temperature is about 85 degrees.

So our hero ventures into the common area in the plaza, where lunchers from a variety of eating emporia have collected to vie for eating space. The Luncher nabs a table for four, the first one that opens up, and within a half a minute an employee queries, "Are you just one? Do you mind if three people use the rest of this table?"

The Luncher replies: "Yes, I do. I'd have taken a small table if there was one."

The employee ignores The Luncher, who is now one-quarter of the way into his McChicken and is wiping mayonnaise from his nose. The mayonnaise has exploded out of the top of the bun. The Luncher is eating quickly, of course, when two women approach his table and one of them, lighting a cigarette, plops down saying, "Is there anybody sitting here?"

"Does it look like it?" responds the irritated Luncher.

"Well, no."

"Are you going to be eating or just smoking?" says The Luncher, noticing that neither woman appears to be engaged in lunch.

"I'm smoking. I'm on a diet. Does the smoke bother you?"

"Well, I don't care for smoke, no."

"So, where do you work?"

"I work for the newspaper."

"Oh, wow, a celebrity! I work for Ash Grove Cement. But I'm really a free-lance writer. I just got the job recently. When I get some time, I'm going to write a book about my divorce. It should be really funny. But first I'm going to marry a really rich man and get him to give me an electric typewriter. Then I'm going to write the book and make a fortune off it. Then I'm going to get rid of the rich husband."

The Luncher wishes her luck as she and her friend head off into the teeming horde of other lunchers now milling in the plaza. But before our hero can finish off his meal, two large gentlemen in pin-striped suits, carrying Big Macs, ask, "Anybody sitting here?"

"Nah," says The Luncher, desperately trying to finish off the McChicken.

"Well," says one Big Mac to the other, "did you see that guy in there who had the winning ticket? Geez, if that happened to me, I'd take the day off."

Says the other Big Mac: "I'd take more than a day off."

The Luncher, gripping his abdomen, hurries out into the street as the two Big Macs turn their conversation to a discussion of income averaging.

For The Luncher, it has been just another typical lunch break, another delectable sampling of the American way of lunch.

She's
the matriarch of
Texas Tom's

Julia Nigro lives in two worlds.

One is genteel, Old World. It is Julia's home in the 500 block of Harrison, where her immigrant parents lived years ago. Stucco walls rise to high ceilings, and archways lead from room to room. Memories fill these chambers in the form of photographs of generations that came after her.

The other world is the shiny stainless-steel interior of a Texas Tom's restaurant on Independence Avenue, a New World kind of place. The seats are a sharp red, the Formica-top tables are smooth and clean. The customers eat fast, the workers work fast, and Julia Nigro labors there amid the bustle.

There is a curious connection between these two worlds, a connection that spans many years and explains how an Italian-American from Kansas City came to be called "Texas Tom" and why Julia Nigro, his mother, still works the lunch hour five days a week at the age of 82.

"My parents were pioneers of the first market here," she says proudly, displaying a photograph of covered wagons, horse-drawn in a circle in muddy Kansas City. Michael and Louise Olivo, her parents, had come from Naples and raised six children here.

"On Saturdays we'd get up at 4 in the morning and work until closing time at 12 at night," Julia says. "I don't forget those times."

At the age of 19, she married Otto Nigro, whose parents had come from Calabria. "They were all hucksters," she says, meaning peddlers of produce. "That's how they made a living. They'd go to Kansas with the wagons. I can hear my father-in-law's voice still."

Otto started out as a huckster but later operated a filling station near the City Market, selling tires and catering to truckers. He eventually bought a truck himself and built a business hauling produce.

By 1943, though, Nigro had become fed up with the trucking business and the headaches it caused him. He got in his Buick and drove toward Texas to collect debts. It was dusk, there was a turn in the road in Oklahoma, and a serviceman crashed into his car. Otto Nigro was dead within months, leaving Julia and her five children alone. The youngest, Tom, was just 5½ years old.

The family struggled for years, surviving on income from a rental property in south Kansas City and from what help the older sons could provide. Young Tom huckstered like his grandfather had. In 1953, when he was 15, he decided to open a dairy bar.

The Nigros bought a prefabricated metal drive-in stand from the Valentine Manufacturing Co. of Wichita and had it hauled to 8401 Winner Road. Tom named the place Frigid Creme, and he, his mother and his future wife, Carmeline, ran the little stand. Business wasn't so hot.

For years they limped along. When business tailed off in the late fall, they closed for the winter, only to start up again when warm weather returned.

One winter, when Tom was working in Mississippi with his brother, a tree trimmer, the two dreamed up a new idea for Tom's drive-in.

"Foot-long hot dogs were very big at the time," says Tom. "So we thought, 'We're going to need a big sandwich that's two-foot long'."

Tom returned to Kansas City, built his own billboard and had it painted. "Texas Tom's Sandwich for Two — longest sandwich in the world," it read. Why "Texas"? Because "Texas" meant big. From that time on, with a drive-in called Texas Tom's and a new product, things improved for Tom Nigro and his family.

The 1960s and '70s saw a proliferation of Texas Tom's restaurants. Relatives and friends bought franchises, and at the height of the business there were 26 outlets in Kansas City, Topeka and several Kansas towns. In 1965 Tom moved the original prefab building to 2619 Independence.

Julia Nigro worked there every day — at Store No. 1. She continued to make the special sauce and breaded steak — her recipes — which became a staple on the Texas Tom's menu.

Later, Tom added to the building and hired more employees. Julia cut back on her hours and duties. But, according to one woman who works there, it takes "something pretty drastic" to keep Julia away from work.

And every day, when work is done, she returns to the source of her strength: home. On Sundays the family gathers there, sometimes as many as 20, to visit her, the matriarch.

Julia greets them with dark brown eyes, graying hair and a firm voice. She is strong in her old age.

From these chambers of Old World style and values, where Julia Nigro receives family and friends, she has looked out on a New World that turned mud into concrete and built the likes of Texas Tom's.

King Cola adds
Royal
Touch
here

Some people say journalism must be a rewarding field because it is so exciting. Others say because it's so interesting. But the real reason journalism is a worthy profession is the hors d'oeuvres.

In what other lines does consideration of the relative merits of stuffed mushrooms (superb, in this case), broccoli (too soggy), deviled eggs (a tad stale), bacon-wrapped liver (nice) and egg rolls (I've had better) add up to a day's work?

Very few.

Journalists, to use a popular term in the bureaucracy, "interface" a lot with the ongoing events of the world. If someone is squashed under a car, the journalist must be on hand to record it. If a balloonist makes it across the Atlantic, a journalist will be there when he comes down.

So, too, when some American magnate decides to launch a new product, a journalist will be on hand to announce it to the world and, perchance, to check out the hors d'oeuvres.

Now these launching ceremonies can be very routine. A few executives will congregate, someone will make a dull speech and the local honcho will pull the veil off the new product. If the business is a substantial one, the mayor will be there to proclaim "Vacuum Cleaner Day" or whatever day is appropriate.

But if the new product is something as essentially useless, delicious, unhealthy and popular as soda pop, watch out! This will be a major product launching affair. The hors d'oeuvres will be better than usual. The mayor will bring his wife.

So it was on Thursday at the swank Carriage Club here. The occasion was the launching of King Cola — a new soda pop in the world.

At the front door were two doormen costumed in medieval shining armor. A marching bagpipe band was warming up for the big climax later on. Inside, visitors to the King Cola spectacular were treated to product specimens by young women, some of whom were encased in giant-size cola cans that served, apparently, as their clothing.

Numerous business, media, advertising and public relations types were on hand, most of them swarming near the hors d'oeuvres tables. A few were hoping to speak to the two principals in the King Cola venture — Chairman of the Board Walter Mack and the local franchise holder, Todd Decker.

Mack, a charming man of 84 who once ruled over Pepsi-Cola, was splendiferous in a navy blue suit with monogrammed handkerchief. While all around him guests bantered with paper crowns atop their heads, Mack calmly outlined his plot against the opposition.

"I'm going to let them have the beach crowd and the surf crowd," he pronounced. "My people are the great American family."

His associate, Todd Decker, though just 22 and brimming with youthful enthusiasm, allowed that he was prepared to drop the entire million-dollar bundle he's invested in the franchise.

"I figured if I held on to the money too long, I'd be reluctant to lose it," he said.

Without further ado, the marching bagpipe band began to play and a ceremonious procession entered the room. It was Queen Elizabeth, right here at the Carriage Club.

Actually, it was Rose Carr of Los Angeles, moonlighting for the Ron Smith Celebrity Lookalike Agency based in Tinsel Town. This was Rose's first gig as queen. She marched regally to a large throne where, after Mayor Richard Berkley pronounced "King Cola Day" in Kansas City, she crowned Decker in a King Cola coronation.

The crowd clapped and those who weren't gulping hors d'oeuvres cheered. Decker flinched. The queen said, "Long Live King Cola."

It all seemed frighteningly appropriate. The royal motif — stretched so far for this product launching — is everywhere in Kansas City. We have the American Royal, the Kansas City Royals, the Hallmark crown, the Kansas City Chiefs. Kansas City and King Cola even have the same initials.

Yet all this was seemingly lost on a St. Louis matron, who spent much of her time staring down the length of her nose. At one point, she commented, "You can be hokey, but you have to be *really* hokey or it will turn out tacky."

Her smile drooped, if only for an instant.

She seemed to be suggesting that the coronation was tacky. Well, perhaps the King Cola coronation will be more discreet in her cadaverous burg. I noticed she seemed to like the hors d'oeuvres here well enough.

An
Empire
of
Joe

Eat at Joe's.

It's a standard line. There are so many Joe's restaurants in the world that "Eat at Joe's" has become a cliche. Everybody's eaten at a Joe's restaurant sometime.

Behind every Joe's restaurant is some Joe. Or at least that's what most people assume. It seems logical. Joe's restaurant. Joe.

But the fact is that "Joe" may really be Billy Ray or Ralph or even Marge. Billy Ray may have bought the joint from Joe years ago.

Most people give no thought to this possibility. To them, Billy Ray must be Joe.

Lou "Joe" Bernstein could tell you about it. He purchased Joe's Servarama restaurant, 75th and Metcalf Avenue, in the late '50s. His name was Lou, but everybody ended up calling him Joe. That was OK by him.

"It was a good deal, and the name stuck," he said.

Mrs. Rose Daffer, owner of Joe's Restaurant at 11102 Blue Ridge Blvd., said every time somebody telephones her restaurant they invariably ask to talk to Joe.

"I tell 'em I'm Joe," she said. No use bucking the tide.

And Willis Harvey, who owns Joe's Restaurant at 75th Street and Holmes Road, said all his customers there call him Joe. Whenever he runs into another Joe's proprietor whose name he has forgotten, "I just call him Joe." Billy Ray doesn't seem to mind.

Under the right circumstances, everybody, it seems, likes to be called Joe. At least by people with money in their wallets. The fact has been well demonstrated in Kansas City.

The city has been blessed with a good number of Joe's restaurants. And while some of them sprang up independently, under the management of some Joe, there is a group here that sprang up under a Jack — John F. "Jack" Byrne. Now an osteopath, Dr. Byrne started about a dozen Joe's restaurants in the '50s. Some died out. None is operated by a Joe now.

Jack's first Joe's was at 39th Street and Indiana Avenue, where the restaurant entrepreneur erected a small restaurant and sold it to J. Oren Elledge (initials J.O.E. — "Joe," get it?). The restaurant featured a bright red sign with "Joe's" written out in script. Dr. Byrne, looking back on it, believes there was something about the color of the sign and the name "Joe's" that made this and subsequent Joe's so popular.

"I couldn't tell you what it was," he said. "But it was a big thing . . . I had all kinds of guys who wanted to buy 'em."

There is something magic about Joe.

But what is it about a Joe's restaurant that makes people want to come in, sit down, say hi to Joe and eat? Dr. Byrne never really knew. He just knew it was a winning formula, so he built a lot of Joe's.

Among those who purchased these Joe's restaurants (in addition to Lou "Joe" Bernstein, Rose "Joe" Daffer and Willis "Joe" Harvey, mentioned above) was Tom "Joe" Gault, who bought a Joe's at 79th and State Line Road in 1956.

Business was good from the start. After all, it was a Joe's.

Years passed and, naturally, most people came to know Tom Gault as Joe. Even his friends, he noticed, would sometimes slip up and call him Joe. But the really confusing thing about Joe's Restaurant & Bar-B-Q, 79th and State Line Road, was that Tom Gault's eldest daughter and office assistant was named Jo.

People would call Joe's and say, "Let me speak to Joe." She'd say, "This is Jo." They'd say, "Is there some other Joe there?" She'd say, "No, I'm the only Jo here." They'd say, "Are you the owner?" She'd say, "No, that's Tom, my father."

Next the caller would want to know if Jo, who is 29, was named after the restaurant or if the restaurant was named after her. "Neither," she'd say. It was just a coincidence.

For Tom Gault, the magic of Joe spawned an empire of Joe. By 1970 he was owner not only of Joe's Restaurant & Bar-B-Q, but also of Joe's Catering and Joe's Barn, a family restaurant in Stanley, Kansas, which seats 1,100.

"A lot of people expected me to name the place after myself — Tom's Barn or something," he said. "But nobody knows me by my name. They know me as Joe. Anybody who runs a place called Joe's for six months or more automatically becomes Joe."

The brand name is transferable. It's practically generic. If Mr. Gault should ever want to sell, a purchaser would be able to step right in as Joe. Anybody can be a Joe, you see. You just have to be flexible.

You just have to be flexible and prepared for confusion should you hire or father somebody named Joe or Jo.

Eat at Joe's — any Joe's.

GOING
TO
EXTREMES

Collector becomes

Art itself

In life, Jim Morgan was an art collector. In death, he became a work of art. The artist, Cork Marcheschi, calls it "contemporary tomb sculpture."

Two electrical transformers power the four phases of the sculpture, which is framed by a 42-by-33-by-12-inch open-faced box. A curtain of metal rods swings rhythmically in front as electric current shinnies up the rods, buzzing and flaring white electric light. A pale-lavender halo flicks on, glowing in the center.

Suddenly a heart-stopping noise sounds, a profound ZAP exploding at the outer edges of a dark clay urn. Within the urn reside the ashes of Jim Morgan, Kansas City art collector.

Startling, even horrifying, the tomb sculpture cannot be ignored. The sculptor believes that art should strike awe in man like lightning does, like death. This piece, which is not on public display, certainly does so. But what did Jim Morgan believe, and why did he choose this course?

No one ever will know for certain why he decided to become a work of art after he died. But a look at the life of this extraordinary man begins to explain.

Just 45 years old at death, Mr. Morgan was a frenetic man, a traveler who committed his life to art. Art is but a vague concept to most. To Jim Morgan it was the supreme, ruling passion.

As a collector of art, he discovered, nurtured and patronized artists all over the country. Inspired by their work, he communicated his inspiration back to them. He plunged into the subculture of American artists and left an indelible mark.

He never was detached. Jim Morgan was a gallery of emotions and a man whose physical appearance changed constantly. "He was a man of many faces," his wife, Myra, said.

Jim Morgan simply changed his face one more time. It was curiously logical that he should become a work of art.

Jim and Myra Morgan were married as teen-agers in the 1950s, Alabama kids whose lives revolved around Jim's art studies at the University of Alabama in Tuscaloosa. It was red-dirt country, beloved country to which Jim Morgan was returning the day he died.

He learned to fly in an officer's training course at the university and, after graduation, became a bomber pilot in the Strategic Air Command. It was ironic that a creative man should become an instrument of destruction. But Jim Morgan viewed it as a duty. And he loved to fly.

The military hitch ended after five years, and Jim Morgan signed up as a TWA pilot. He moved to Kansas City in 1964 with his wife and three kids. Thus began the convenient arrangement that set the pattern of his life.

It was simple, really. The art buff only flew airplanes so he could get to his art. Layovers in cities provided opportunities to visit studios and galleries, meet artists, talk and buy.

His collection began to grow. So did his children, and, 12 years ago, Myra Morgan decided to open her own gallery. She became a dealer, a businesswoman. But her husband, too restless to work regular hours or even to sit still for very long, persisted in his odyssey of art.

It may have been the tempo of his life, or it may have been in his genes. For whatever reason, Jim Morgan was stricken by a massive heart attack seven years ago, shortly after he had landed a jet in Denver. A heart bypass operation followed. Arteriosclerosis was diagnosed.

Jim Morgan was in bad shape. And he was scared.

He began to make provisions for his own death. He wrote out the details of his memorial service. And he asked a friend, sculptor Cork Marcheschi, to build him an electrical tomb.

"Jim told me that after his bypass operation he was having nightmares about dying, that he wanted to get his affairs in order," Mr. Marcheschi recalled. "There never was any explanation other than that this piece would give him some peace."

The sculptor was reluctant. But the collector was a great friend, "one of the best things that ever happened to me." Mr. Morgan implored him to construct the work. He complied.

With death looking over his shoulder, Jim Morgan began to live even more intensely. He was an Olympic traveler who scribbled quotations such as "The end is nothing. The road is all." He swapped flying for a BMW touring motorcycle.

On April 17, at 9:18 a.m., Jim Morgan's motorcycle hit a concrete divider on Interstate 70 near St. Louis. He appeared to slump in his seat just before the bike veered out of the center lane.

Finally, according to his wishes, the art collector realized his destiny in the smooth lines of pottery and the angry whine of electric current.

Kansas City's most
Happy Fella

If you're looking for something positive to consider, you might want to talk with A.F. "Al" Estensen, a gentleman of nearly 80 years who distributes positive information everywhere he goes.

In fact, he might talk to you before you get a chance to talk to him.

Such was the case a few nights ago in a midtown Safeway store, where Al was in the checkout line. As usual, he had his fliers, pamphlets, handouts, prayer sheets and whatnot with him. He set the stuff down on the conveyor belt, shuffling his papers just as if he were at the office. He handed a customer a sheet that advises:

"LADIES DON'T SMOKE — AND NEITHER DO GENTLE-MEN. CIGARETTES CONTAMINATE YOUR BLOOD AND UNDERMINE YOUR HEALTH."

The checkout clerk told Al he couldn't hand out information in the grocery store. So Al, as he usually does, replied that in fact he had that right under the U.S. Constitution. Then he smiled.

It was a typical encounter for a man who wants to let people consider the positive side of life. Al Estensen is quite possibly the most optimistic man in Kansas City.

In a recent conversation at his home, Al looked me in the eye with his penetrating, twinkling stare and declared: "I'm not a distributor of information. I do it only as I go about my daily routine, whether it be grocery shopping, getting gas or in conversation — amiable conversation.

"This is the essence of my effort — to promote the principles of the U.S. Constitution, to emphasize the rules that have made our country the greatest country in the history of the Earth.

"And I am a believer in good health, which is why I say to ladies: Do not smoke! And that includes gentlemen, too."

Al told a story of meeting a man in a grocery store and admonishing him to quit smoking. The man replied, "How am I going to quit smoking?"

Al led the man to a shelf of nuts.

"I gave him an almond nut," Al relates. " 'Instead of reaching for that cigarette,' I told him, 'reach for an almond nut and start masticating until pretty soon you'll forget smoking!' "

Al speaks in eloquent exclamations. And nothing in his vocabulary of good news gets more emphasis than the Rosedale Optimist Youth Camp and Lodge, in Cassville, Missouri. Al is the director of the camp and a longstanding member of the Optimist Club of Rosedale!

Much of the material Al has printed up over the years relates to the uplifting of youth through better health care, the virtues of horseshoe pitching ("For 2,000 years our forebears have been pitching horseshoes — 100 years before Christ," he says. "Think of it!") and good fresh air.

Al got plenty of good fresh air himself growing up on a farm in South Dakota. But being an optimistic man, he wanted to "see the world. I wanted to see California!" In 1920, he set out to do so.

Arriving in San Jose when it was just a punk town, Al had the good fortune to start his own automobile service station. Estensen Motor Service succeeded, in part, because Al had a talent as a pamphleteer. He recalls showering and shaving every night before bedtime so that at 3 a.m. he could rise and hit the streets of San Jose to distribute his literature.

"I spread the pamphlet — Lubricate Your Car! — up one street and down another," he remembers. "By 6 o'clock, when I opened up, I would have business ready to go."

Inspired by the constitutional freedoms that allowed him to pass out information and run his own business, Al Estensen in 1942 published at his own cost 30,000 copies of the U.S. Constitution. He distributed them to California school children and elected officials. He still distributes Constitutions.

Upon retiring, Al came to Kansas City, the birthplace of his wife, the former Louise Tobler. Louise's family operates Tobler's Flowers Inc., so Al wrote up a "Tribute to the Flower and the Bee" which reads, in part:

"The Almighty God, the Creator, designed the blade of grass, the plant, the flower, the bee, the honey bee, before man appeared on the earth together with all of his adornments; therefore, the flower, the acme of color and beauty, could be the first honor present to lift the spirit and to glorify the grace, charm, character and life of men, women and children everywhere."

And so Al Estensen, in his various ways, continues to deliver his message — an optimistic man.

Barkeeper is a
Thug
for
Charity

It's a funny thing about Joe's Standard Bar, 412 E. 14th Terrace. Most of the customers come out with their arms twisted and hanging loosely from the socket.

Behind the bar a fellow called Notzie Rotolo chomps on big cigars. He's the one who twists all the arms. You'd think the customers would abandon his joint. But they don't. They like the way this guy Notzie works them over.

"If you don't donate," one customer says, "you don't drink."

So what is this? An influence racket? Some kind of extortion scheme? Well, sort of.

Behind the bar a fellow called Notzie Rotolo chomps on big cigars and takes in money for the retarded, the palsied, the brain damaged, the afflicted.

And yes, he uses some muscle on his customers and suppliers. He takes their money to cover for drinks and food. Then he takes some more for people who really need it.

Notzie Rotolo is a gangster of love.

His customers and suppliers don't seem to mind. Says J.D. Walker, a customer and Missouri mental health official: "His good customers give him a twenty for a beer, and he gives them no change. He says, 'Thanks, you just contributed to cerebral palsy.' You'd think they'd run, but they don't."

Mr. Rotolo explains, "It makes 'em feel good to give." But there's more to it than that.

It has something to do with Notzie Rotolo, the man. His bar glitters with Christmas decor all year around. Humorous sayings, pungent aphorisms concerning the human condition, unprintable expletives and obscure mementos fill the place. On Fridays women customers get free flowers. The food is cheap and good.

And in the middle of all this stands Notzie Rotolo, a round-faced guy who looks a little like Art Buchwald with thick, black-rimmed glasses. Born on Columbus Day, eminently proud that he was named the Knights of Columbus Man of the Year in 1976, Mr. Rotolo is a warm-spirited and intense man whose establishment has become a social gathering place and informal fund-raising agency.

Inherited from his Uncle Joe Cassata after World War II, Joe's Standard Bar has been a fixture in the neighborhood since 1935. But perhaps the most important event in that time was the birth of Notzie and Vita Rotolo's daughter Vicki 22 years ago.

Vicki was born profoundly retarded, deprived of oxygen when her umbilical cord became twisted around her throat. She was taken to area hospitals where conflicting diagnoses were made. Her parents, caught in a dilemma all too common 20 years ago, didn't know what to do with her.

"I couldn't find help no place," Mr. Rotolo says. "There was nothing around here at the time."

Vita Rotolo remembers, "They said, 'Take her home and learn to live with it.'"

But the Rotolos wouldn't accept such bleak counsel. Friends say the barkeeper and his wife kept trying to find a "cure" for their daughter.

It was a Roman Catholic priest who finally helped the Rotolos accept their plight. Notzie Rotolo asked the priest to pray for Vicki, and the priest said, "No, ask Vicki to pray for us. Vicki is an angel."

And perhaps she is. It was because of her that Notzie Rotolo, in his desperate searching, found Ed Minter, then-director of the United Cerebral Palsy Association of Greater Kansas City. Mr. Minter placed Vicki in a day-care center, although she did not suffer cerebral palsy. In gratitude, Mr. Rotolo began to raise money for the organization's annual Christmas party.

"They were giving out a tie or a handkerchief for a gift," Mr. Rotolo recalls. "So I said, 'That ain't no good.' So I started mooching from my customers." That first year Notzie Rotolo turned his customers' contributions into billfolds, each containing $2. "After that it was radios, watches, binoculars."

Vicki Rotolo was placed in the Higginsville State School 10 years ago and now Mr. Rotolo raises money and obtains gifts for the school, the cerebral palsy organization and the Knights of Columbus annual "Christmas in September" party.

The barkeeper became a dynamic fund-raiser for the retarded and developmentally disabled, raising thousands of dollars and filling funding gaps through sheer resourcefulness. And he became a man to whom many turn.

Duane Hensley, director of the Missouri Department of Mental Health from 1976 to 1979, recalls: "All I had to do was call Joe's Standard Bar and say, 'Hey, Notzie, I got some kids who need clothes,' or, 'Hey, Notzie, I've got some kids who want to go on a camping trip.' And he'd come up with what I needed."

He'd twist arms for it.

The Market is
Bullish
on
Kids

The recent news that a New Jersey couple allegedly tried to sell their 14-month-old son for an $8,800 used Corvette came as a complete shock to me.

I had no idea a child was worth that much. If I had some of my own, I might be tempted to unload them for a new BMW. Let's face it, in today's economy parents can't afford to keep their kids — especially when they're worth so much in the car market.

Look at the facts. Just bringing a child into the world will cost you almost $2,000 in hospital and doctor's fees (you can get a VW bug in pretty good shape for that). Then you have to feed it, clothe it and stay with it all the time (which means keeping an index file of baby sitters' names, not to mention paying them outrageous fees).

When Junior gets old enough to speak, he'll start asking for things: a ray gun, a tricycle, an erector set, cherry bombs, a BB gun, a sled, a real bicycle, a Darth Vader helmet. The list goes on and on. By the time Junior is old enough to go to college (assuming you haven't sold him yet), he will have asked for thousands of dollars worth of destructible junk. How much he gets depends on how much you've got.

I don't know what the bottom line is on bringing a child to maturity, but with tuition, books, clothing, bail bond money, the car and lost earning years off your own life, surely the tally comes to a heck of a lot more than $8,800.

So no wonder parents are tempted to sell their kids. It's the fiscally responsible thing to do.

Moreover, thinking a little harder on the subject, it occurs to me that now just might be the optimal time to sell children. The market is bullish on kids.

There are no market analysts who will verify this impression for me, but here's my own analysis of why the New Jersey couple apparently were able to cut such a good deal and why the future may bring only lower prices for children.

The abortion debate. Trying to take a detached, rational view of the debate over abortion, it seems to me the anti-abortionists are slowly gaining ground. Federal financing for abortion has been restricted and "Right to Life" groups are finding they have increased political clout.

Primary result: More children. Secondary result: Lower prices for children. While the price of Corvettes will no doubt continue to soar, the exchange value for little Johnny inevitably will go down. That's simple economics.

The baby boom's babies. After 10 years of searching out their own "personal space," postwar babies now are reportedly settling down to have babies of their own. That means a new bulge in the population growth rate.

Result: Same as above. One additional note is appropriate here: It may be anticipated that the children of the liberated may themselves be more desirous of liberation. Hence these children may be more likely to acquiesce in their sale. However, this is mere speculation.

The clone syndrome. Some scientists tell us that cloning of human beings may not be far off.

Primary result: More kids, lower prices. Secondary result: This may mean the reorganization of the entire child market. For one thing, the buyer — instead of being subject to product availability and fluctuations in quality control — will be in a position to order a child according to specifications. You want a redhead, you got a redhead.

Buying a child will become a lot like buying a Corvette. You could pay more for all the options or you could stick with the basic model. You probably could get a deal on a showroom model.

As has happened in other high-technology fields, America will at first dominate the international child market. This will drive prices up initially, but once the Japanese and West Germans catch up, foreign competition will bring prices right back down.

Fewer buyers. Logically enough, with more children in the world there will be fewer parents without children.

Result: the bottom is likely to drop out of the child business. The scenario, for kid merchants, is grim. The supply increases and diversifies, the demand decreases and the world is left with a glut of children for sale.

Can you image the horror of it? Fast-talking radio voices advertising clearinghouse sales — buy now, pay later! Children growing old in warehouses . . .

There can be little doubt. Now is the time to consider selling your children. In times like these — when a 14-month-old male will bring in a 1977 Corvette — you have to admit the price is right.

Just tell Junior he's going on vacation.

Mr.
Miscellaneous
relaxes at
Home

As you head east on 27th Street past Benton, the view is fairly predictable until you get to Jimmy Green's place. There, you sense a change in the landscape . . .

It's either the electric clock on the front of his painted red-brick house, or the U.S. flags front and back, or the lustrous shining globes, or the pink and yellow bird statues, the lawn furniture and umbrellas.

Or maybe it's the six-hole putting course in the back, or the signs bearing the names of Jimmy's former loves, or the plastic flowers, or the gargoyles, or the "I'm For Real" sign on the garage, or the bars on the windows, the pink railings on the sidewalk.

Or perhaps it's Jimmy's motto in several places front and back: "It's So Nice to Be Nice."

On the other hand, it could be what's inside that gives Green's house a slightly different flavor from the others on the block.

Could it be the Hawaiian bamboo hut inside his den, complete with bar and bottle of J&B? Or the photographs of nude women plastered all over the walls?

Conceivably, it's the buzzers, intercoms and telephones in every nook of the place, or the wrought-iron musical instruments garnishing the walls, or the rock garden/water fountain in the front foyer, or the four-poster bed with suspended television attachment, or the Angela Davis posters, or even the vibrator table in the penthouse.

Or maybe what's really different about this place is Jimmy Green himself.

Sixty-three years old, this man was once a dashing Army sergeant, say the photographs on his walls. His women were beautiful and numerous, his travels long and diverse.

From the shores of New Guinea in the South Pacific to the nudist colonies of California to the stately Indian Hills Country Club in Kansas City, Jimmy Green left his mark.

His life is more sedate now.

He pads around his home in sneakers and a jumpsuit. He takes his heart medicine. His chest bears the savage scars of two open-heart

144

operations. His belly is pocked by a gunshot wound. He lives on Army disability pay because the war in the Pacific left him shell-shocked.

"I've forgotten more about life than most men ever knew," says Jimmy. His hair is flecked with gray now, his face thin.

Jimmy's story began in the East Texas town of Texarkana. His boss, an Italian who owned a shine parlor, talked always of Kansas City, a great city to the north. At the age of 15, Jimmy came here.

His first job was as a bar porter at Wolf's Tavern, 18th and Vine. He met Count Basie and Jimmy Rushing there and had himself a good time in the '30s. World War II found Green in the Army, shipped out to the South Pacific, where he was a member of an amphibious landing unit.

He served in several other capacities — quartermaster, cook, instructor — and was discharged a sergeant.

Jimmy returned to Kansas City after the war and landed a great job as maitre d' at the Indian Hills Country Club. He catered private parties at the club and worked other jobs on the side through the late '40s and into the '50s.

"I was young and I was smart. I wanted to see how many jobs I could do," he remembers.

At the height of his money-making career in those days, Jimmy was earning $150 a week. By about 1950 he had put away enough to lay down $2,500 for the house at 3107 E. 27th.

From the very beginning, Jimmy took good care of his house. He began to accumulate things quickly. He bought from Sears and the Jones Store and furniture stores on Troost. "Anyplace I'd go, if I'd see something I liked, I'd buy it," he says.

He bought enormous amounts of stuff. He clipped photographs from magazines and took hundreds of his own pictures. His walls display the yellowed tokens of the 1940s and the psychedelic art of the 1960s alike.

"I've got so much stuff, I can't explain it all," he laments.

But in 1957, a bullet slowed Jimmy Green down. A robber shot him outside his home. Between the bullet wound and the memories of combat, Jimmy lost his health. He suffered a nervous breakdown and came under the care of a Veterans Administration psychiatrist.

Since that time, Jimmy has regained his balance but has been plagued by heart trouble. Retired and recuperating from the open-heart surgery, he spends his days taking care of the house.

He moves some of his things inside at night, then outside again in the morning. He changes the arrangements with the seasons — bird baths give way to Santa Clauses. He gets his exercise this way. Souvenirs of a lifetime's experiences surround him on his corner lot.

"I look out on the sidewalk," he says, "and I see people breaking into the grocery store. I see the hookers walking along. I see people that talk to themselves."

But it doesn't get Jimmy down. He still believes "It's So Nice to Be Nice." And he still reads the Sears catalog.

Charting
a house of
Cards

C. P. Dewey is worried about America.

"There's got to be some way to tell the people, to tell the country how bad things are before it gets too far," he says as he unrolls his chart.

It is a rather long chart, actually.

C. P. Dewey is unrolling it in the dining room of his home, and by the time the chart is completely spread out, it has run through his living room and all the way to the front door.

The chart depicts growth in the national debt, from the administration of George Washington to the administration of Jimmy Carter. The reason the thing is more than 30 feet long is that the national debt is more than $825 billion and on its way to $1 trillion. Each billion dollars is represented on Mr. Dewey's chart by one-half inch of red magic marker.

That's a lot of red.

But back up a minute here. This is a story about economics, and since nobody, including C. P. Dewey, can make a whit of sense out of economics, let's begin with a concrete description of Mr. Dewey and his chart.

Mr. Dewey is a robust 70-year-old man with silver-white hair, bright blue eyes and bushy eyebrows that suggest an inquisitive nature. Retired from nearly 50 years of employment by various government agencies, he lives on a pension and Social Security payments. He and his wife maintain an attractive home in Kansas City.

Mr. Dewey wears a handsome, light-colored tweed suit that makes him look a little like a college professor. He has a large dog, which he thoughtfully banishes to the basement when visitors arrive.

There is nothing terribly unusual about C. P. Dewey. He doesn't claim to be brilliant, or even smart, but he has a good eye for absurdity and a hearty laugh to match.

His chart is somewhat unusual, however. It is fashioned out of a long roll of brown corrugated paper with white stock laid on top. Mr. Dewey keeps it rolled up and shows it only on special request.

At the far left (the beginning) of the chart are the names of the presidents written in a column about 2 feet tall. Originating alongside each name is a horizontal red line that represents the national debt at five-year intervals.

The lines next to such presidents as Washington, Jefferson and Andrew Jackson are minuscule, showing figures well below a billion dollars. In order to see how much money the government owed under Franklin D. Roosevelt, however, Mr. Dewey must unroll the first 10 feet of the chart.

To see what the government owes under Jimmy Carter, the chart must be unrolled completely — which is almost impossible in C. P. Dewey's house.

To fill in the blank spaces above the interminably long red lines of recent administrations, Mr. Dewey has laid out all 139 pages of a book he says begins to explain what these dollars mean. The book, written by E. F. Schumacher, is called *A Guide For the Perplexed.*

Stenciled in over these 139 pages is the title of Dewey's chart, which could be read from a very great distance: "Collage and graph depicting how a great nation spends itself out of debt and a solution to this dilemma: Economics for people not for products."

Dewey completed his chart by laying clear plastic over the corrugated paper, the white stock, the lines and the book pages. Then he rolled it up and waited for someone to come by and ask him:

Why did you do this, C. P. Dewey?

His answer, boiled down, is this: The United States is caught in a rampaging inflationary spiral. Americans are spending far more than they should on obscure, unnecessary products. They drive when they should walk. Everyone in the family works so they can pay rising prices for things they don't really need.

And underpinning all this dollar drain is the national debt, the total of all government debts to its citizens, industry, employees, etc., etc. The national debt, which Dewey says was $75.4 million in 1790, is now more than $825 billion, and every year Congress raises the ceiling to allow for more.

To pay interest on the securities it sells, the government goes out and sells some more. It's a house of cards and everyone, including C. P. Dewey, hopes it won't fall down.

After completing the chart, Dewey considered taking it down to the Federal Reserve Bank in Kansas City and unrolling it on the sidewalk. But he was afraid he would be arrested. He thought about renting a storefront on 12th so he could hang the thing up.

He wants people to see it, to get a concrete idea of how large the house of cards has grown. "I did it so people could see what is happening to America," he says. "It is astounding."

C. P. Dewey turned 21 the day after the stock market crashed, and he spent his adult life balancing ledgers. Now, in his retirement years, he is trying to do something about America's economic plight. He is confused and worried, and he is certainly not alone.

I know
It's
incredible,
but, . . .

These certainly are hyped-up days. Nobody is satisfied unless he's hearing the absolute latest, most up-to-date, most incredible information around.

Television shows featuring once-credible personalities are soaring up the ratings charts by offering "incredible," "real" information. Grocery store tabloids continue to sell millions of copies by giving their readers the best info on disease control, head transplants for monkeys, movie-star romances and outer-space communications.

We seem to have a fascination for this slightly stilted form of gossip. Anything incredible, new, terrific or revealing is gobbled up by the public. Fiction is touted as fact. Facts are touted as stranger than fiction. Both are used to sell foot powder and arthritis pills.

Yet, as the flow of this incredible information becomes faster and ever more incredible, people become adjusted to constant exposure to incredible information. Just as fiction becomes fact, incredible information becomes trivial. After all, how many times can you, in tones of utter amazement, say "That's incredible"?

With the explosion of incredible information, what becomes important is not how inherently incredible something actually is, but the manner in which the information is communicated.

If you breathe something into someone's ear, it may come across as completely incredible. For example: "Pssst, have you heard? *Most of the catfish in Troost Lake are tiny.*"

This kind of information, when presented in the appropriate fashion, comes across as, yes, truly incredible. It can make you quake in your boots and want to turn on the television set or go out and buy the *National Enquirer.*

On the other hand, if the exact same information were passed along casually, as though it were no big deal, like, "Hey, most of the catfish in Troost Lake are tiny," then there's nothing at all incredible about it, is there?

To demonstrate the incredulity principle, here is some information that is terrific, revealing and amazing. It may not strike you as such right off the bat. But if you read it correctly — maybe whisper it to yourself or shout it at the top of your lungs — you'll agree that it is, indeed, incredible, if you think it is . . .

The eternal flame atop the Liberty Memorial is a fake.

Texas Tom's fast-food chain was started by an Italian-American from Kansas City.

The Who came to town and nobody got stomped to death.

A New York columnist called Biba's in Kansas City the wildest disco in Kansas.

Mr. and Mrs. C. Ridgely Harrison returned recently from the Caribbean, where they reportedly fished for snapper, grouper, bonefish and tarpon.

"The Last of the Blue Devils," a documentary film about Kansas City jazz, starring a Kansas City bartender and made by a sometime Kansas Citian, is a smash in Boston and London.

Cockfighting is legal in Kansas.

A peanut farmer and a former movie star are the front-runners in the presidential campaign.

Timothy Leary is earning a living as a stand-up comic.

There is an epitaph in Council Bluffs, Iowa, that reads:

I told you I was sick
Now do you believe me?

Jaroldine White placed an ad in *The Kansas City Star* to tell her friends that her telephone was back in service.

The International Marriage Bureau here has announced that it can tell you who you are and what your goals are.

The last mayoral election in Kansas City was between an envelope magnate and a mortician. The mortician lost.

Hundreds of people in the metro area recently competed to be named ugliest bartender in town.

Johnson County is named after a pro-slavery missionary who ripped off the Indians. Wyandotte County is named after the Indians.

A poll taken in Europe once showed that the three best-known Americans were Mark Twain, Jesse James and Mickey Mouse — all Missourians.

Kansas is most famous for its ground and its air.

The mayor of Westport weighs more than 300 pounds.

Most of the catfish in Troost Lake are . . .

Ah, but you've heard that one already, haven't you? Better leave it at that. It's not good to overdose on incredible information, and you've had plenty for one sitting.

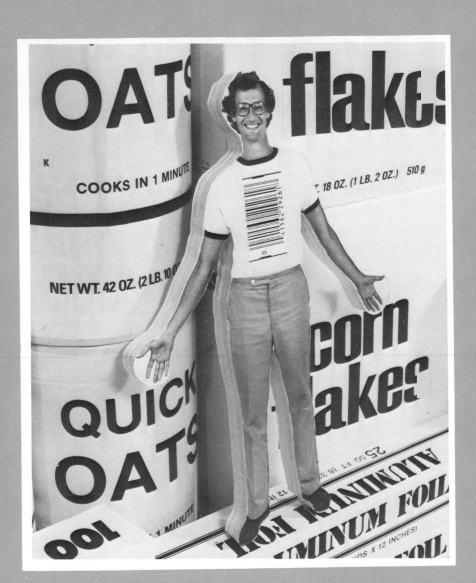

HIGH
ANXIETY

He thought he was a
Cocker
Spaniel

What's in a name? A lot is, I'll tell you. Just ask any kid called *Follingsworth.*

A name can make a difference. Imagine you've just been born, and, before you can even form a word of protest, your parents sock you with *Cyrus* or *Spottswood* or *Jehosephat.*

Thereafter follows a lifetime of explanation or, if you're lucky, a nickname that sticks.

Now I can't say I have experienced the worst myself. *Arthur* is an acceptable appellation, I suppose. Not too bad. But it could have been a lot better.

Oh, the usual reasons were offered. "Your grandfather was named *Arthur,* and so you will be too. If you don't like it we'll ring up the orphanage."

So *Arthur* it was.

But like a lot of *Spottswoods* and *Hymans* I always had this feeling that life would be somehow better were I named *Jimmy* or *Chuck* or *Jim Bob* or some such. Girls would respond more favorably. Teachers wouldn't have such substantial syllables with which to reproach me: "A-a-a-r-r-thur, where IS your homework?"

Besides, nobody ever spelled the name correctly. It was always *Arther, Authur, Aurthur* or *Aurther.*

Being named *Arthur* placed me in that segment of society — a minority, you understand — that pronouces its name to itself and thinks, "If only they had named me *Ralph.* Anything but *Horatio."*

My only consolation lay in the great tradition of King Arthur, whose magical accomplishment with the sword in the stone gave me hope for a better, even a royal, future. But such fantasies were obliterated by the cold light of reason. No matter how I construed it, a throne in my future seemed unlikely. ("A-a-a-r-r-thur, come fetch your scepter"??? I thought it improbable.)

Granted, my friends were kind. They didn't seem to consider *Arthur* too peculiar. They called me *Artie* or *Art.* But in my heart of hearts, I thought something was wrong with my name.

The notion was reinforced by *Mad* magazine, a humorous publication that I read devotedly as a child. *Mad* artists placed curious little drawings in the margins of their features, and one of their regular marginal characters was a potted plant called *Arthur*. Arthur was always falling off ledges or being doused with too much water. I felt vaguely insulted by the hapless plant. Why didn't they call it *Mike?*

The years passed and I discovered there were other *Arthurs* in the world, *Arthurs* of substance: Arthur Schlesinger, the historian; Arthur Koestler, the writer; Arthur Godfrey, the radio personality; Art Garfunkel, the singer. But for every step forward, it seemed there was always a step back.

There was, for example, the strange case of Mel Brooks and his movie, "High Anxiety." Sitting there in the theater, I was initially pleased to learn that a central character in the film was called not just *Arthur,* but *Arthur Brisbane, the industrialist.*

However, I was dismayed to observe this *Arthur Brisbane, the industrialist,* in the violent ward of a mental institution functioning under the delusion that he was a cocker spaniel. This was a setback.

My sister wrote away to Mel Brooks for an explanation, but all she received in return was an 8-by-10-inch glossy photo signed, "Best, Mel." Thanks to Mel I was back at square one, with the *Chaunceys* and *Spottswoods* and *Bainbridges* and *Millards.* Some years passed.

And then all of a sudden, it seemed a new day was dawning for *Arthur.* There was a movie out called "Arthur" and it was a hit. All over America people were watching comedian Dudley Moore portray a guy named *Arthur* who seemed to have the world on a string. Rich, happy, in love — this *Arthur* had it all. Sure, he was a drunk, but a nice drunk.

And then there was the title song of the movie "Arthur." It was a hit, too. The *Chucks* of the world can have no idea what it's like for an *Arthur* to hear "his" song on the radio constantly.

The movie and song, I became convinced, represented a turning point in the modern history of the name. Henceforth, *Arthur* would become a mainstream moniker — something parents would bestow upon their kids with no subsequent grousing. The movie "Arthur" was, I felt, a great public relations coup.

So I was not surprised to learn that Steve Martin, in his new movie, "Pennies From Heaven," plays a fellow called *Arthur Parker.*

For his very first non-comedic role, Steve Martin chose to be an *Arthur.* This was highly significant.

It appears now that the worst is over for the *Arthurs* of the world. I can only hope that someday the *Spottswoods,* the *Hymans* and the *Horatios* will be privileged to say the same.

Ogre
status isn't
Easy
to attain

'Tis the season for children, or so the noise level on my block tells me. But what is the proper thing to do about these swarms of urchins? Be nice? Or be an ogre?

One could be nice and smile while the little ones run screaming over one's lawn, trampling flowers and beating down base paths where grass once grew. Or one could be an ogre and snarl menacingly so no child ever dares set foot in the ogre's lair.

It is so difficult to know what to do. The world is full enough of ogres, without one more. But is it possible, could it be, that it is children who make all the ogres?

I don't have the answers. All I know is that for the last few months I have watched with trepidation the activity on a neighboring block. There, near a schoolyard, large groupings of small children have banded together to romp in a youthful crusade from one end of the block to another, pitching balls, screaming wantonly and hopping over porch rails. They resemble a herd of animals but for their high-pitched squeals and colorful clothing.

With the beginning of summer not far off, I now find that the child-activity index is up everywhere, not just on the neighboring block. The kiddies are running amok on my block too. And yours as well, no doubt.

The other night I came home from work, as most ogres do, about 6 p.m. I made a fine picture of adult dismay as I sat at my dining-room table quaffing a beer and letting my shoulders slump after a long day of holding them up.

But the tranquility was suddenly interrupted by a small squadron of whippersnappers storming across my porch, heaving their tiny bodies over first one rail and then the other.

A game of hide and seek, I gathered, was the cause of the tempest.

I listened, feigning bemusement, as the corps hurtled down the walkway next to my house. I listened, feigning bemusement, as a large girl of about 10 collided with the side of my house. I listened, feigning bemusement, as the heavy sounds of light feet stomped once more across my front porch.

I pondered the matter of childhood.

Surely, I thought to myself, we all go through it. We all scream and carry on. We throw rocks, break windows, wreak havoc.

And surely, as children, we all fear and detest adult ogres. The ogres are the worst of humanity, in a child's eyes. This I remember well enough from my own chldhood, even as I sat in adult dismay feeling the ogre in me getting ready to introduce himself.

I remembered the great ogre, Mr. Fink. That was truly his name; this is not a lie. Mr. Fink lived on the other side of my friend's fence, the fence we used for our makeshift ballpark. Being ballplayers, we sometimes had occasion to hit a home run into Mr. Fink's yard. Mr. Fink hated this, and we knew it.

But baseballs cost a dollar at least, and no self-respecting kid could allow one to be lost to the yard of even the greatest ogre. So, my friend or I would have to dash into Mr. Fink's yard, grab the ball and run away shuddering as Mr. Fink's booming voice blew cold air across our backs. He was a great ogre, Mr. Fink.

I thought of him hard as the children ripped through my rose bush, one shouting, "One-two-three-four-five-six-seven-eight-nine-10. Ready or not here I come!"

Suddenly unable to control myself, I stormed from my table, shoulders thrown back, ogre's blood coursing through my throbbing veins. I yanked open the front door, planted my feet on the front porch and this is what I said:

"Flee, children, flee. Stop making such a racket!"

The children stopped dead in their tracks and looked at me. They were small children, awfully small. There was a kind of dull confusion in their eyes. An ogre was screaming at them to "flee."

Looking back on it now, I suppose small children don't know the word "flee." I really don't know why I used it. The children looked so pathetic standing there while I was shouting at them to flee.

They didn't actually run away as I expected them to. They just stood around. I turned to go back into my house and, as I did, I heard one boy say to the others, "I think he wants us to stay off the porch."

I appreciated that. There's always one "good" kid in the lot who knows what adults are trying to say when they say things that don't seem to make any sense.

Back inside, I tried to put the incident into perspective. From somewhere in my genetic makeup an ogre had emerged, but not a very effective ogre. The children weren't even scared.

Well, I supposed, Mr. Fink must have been a rookie ogre once, too.

Agri-idiots

can farm in the city

The Perfect Idiot's Guide to Farming, or at Least Gardening, in the Modern City.

I have fantasies that someday soon I'll write a book with a title such as this. I can't imagine the book will have much success, however, based as it is upon a lack of information rather than a wealth of it. Yet, who knows? Many authors are not restrained by their ignorance.

Certainly my credentials are good. No experience farming whatsoever — unless you count a tour through a dairy barn when I was 7 years old. No real notion of food products at all — except those wrapped in plastic at the supermarket.

Virtually no family background in agriculture — the last member of my family to earn a living on the farm was my great-great-grandfather, whose son fled the fields for a career in social utopianism.

With these credentials, I feel certain there are a lot of non-farmers out there who would relate well to me as an author.

What would I put in this book? Oh, personal experience mostly. I think I would start the book off with an apologia, which is a common practice among authors who, though ignorant in their field, decide to write the book anyway. My apologia would say something like this:

"Though Kansas City is well-known as an American 'breadbasket,' there are nevertheless residents of this city who are surprisingly unschooled in the subject of agriculture. These are urban citizens who couldn't tell a field of soybeans from a field of corn. My book will not help urbanites make such fine distinctions, but seeks merely to provide them with suitable reading material for their coffee tables.
— The Author."

That said, I think I would then plunge into the basics of starting your own farm, or garden, in the modern city. What are the necessaries?

Well, the urban farmer will need the Big Four, even for the most basic spread. These are: (No. 1) sunlight, (No. 2) water, (No. 3) dirt, and (No. 4) plants.

Concerning No. 4, the perfect idiot has the option of using seeds (as opposed to plants), but plants are more impressive if your farm should suddenly die. At least, you can point to the dead plants and say something like, "The 'hoppers got 'em." With seeds lying dead in the dirt, nobody will even know you had a farm.

What kind of plants should the urban farmer grow?

You should grow food that you like to eat. There's no sense in harvesting bushels of Brussels sprouts if you don't like to eat them. I happen to like them, so I planted a small patch this year.

You can also grow tomatoes, squash, lettuce, peppers or whatever. If it tastes good, put it in the ground and see what happens. Just be sure the rest of the Big Four is present in the right balance: Not too much of No. 2 without enough of No. 3 and vice versa. Don't plant your farm under a porch, because you'll need lots of No. 1.

And, most important, don't worry too much. The stuff usually grows no matter what you do.

See how easy it is to farm? Even a perfect idiot, living in the city, can have his own farm, or at least a garden. But what about insects, you say, and farm-eating rodents?

I really don't know much about insects and rodents. It has occurred to me that birds might be a problem as well. Recently, I noticed holes in some of the plants on my farm and got to wondering what was responsible for them.

I studied the crops closely and walked up and down both rows many times. I was very concerned and feared that my bumper crop was in the process of being bumped off. But I never did see anything nibbling. I saw quite a few lightning bugs at night, but they seemed so innocent.

With a similar insect or pest problem, I recommend the urban farmer do what I ended up doing: March down to a local nursery or hardware store and purchase the nastiest-looking pesticide on the shelf.

And that should do it, urban farmer.

Enough of the Big Four in the right amounts, a good killer pesticide, a growing season free of tornadoes, and you should have a super harvest by the fall. You can become a successful farmer in spite of yourself.

That's what I would put in *The Perfect Idiot's Guide to Farming, or at Least Gardening, in the Modern City*. But I probably won't have time to write it this year, what with the farm and all.

Saying
it with
Gimmicks

gimmick (gim'ik) *n*. 1. (Colloq.) a tricky device — *Webster's Dictionary*
Gimmicks. What a plague on moral man!

It seems one can't take a step without coming across some form of gimmick, doodad, contrivance or other attention-getting ploy.

Instead of furthering the cause of humanity, men and women of intelligence or craft devote themselves entirely to devising elaborate new ways of distracting each other.

No automobile is complete without a bumper sticker. No eyeglass may lack a monogram. No drink is tasty without some Polynesian moniker like *Fiji fruit flip.* No pant leg is adequate without the current curve or the latest flare, the classy cuff or the tightest fit.

☆ ☆ ☆ ☆ ☆ ☆ ☆ ☆ ☆ ☆ ☆ ☆ ☆ ☆

Why is this? you ask. It is, simply, the fruit of a whole history of gimmickry, beginning with the discovery of the wheel.

Man trundled from cave to field, hunting and multiplying in the most elementary, untricky fashion for thousands of years.

But was that good enough?

Noooooo. Some genius had to invent the wheel and get the tradition of gimmickry rolling. From the first, cave-dwelling elders could see what would happen. The wheel would undermine the virtue of patient, steady work. No one would want to walk anywhere anymore, or carry anything on his back. They'd want to wheel all over the place.

The wheel brought the first hot-rodders and it's been downhill since then. Think of every drive-in this and drive-out that, every boxed hamburger and ad jingle and all the **backseat pregnancies** and you begin to understand the wheel-gimmick legacy.

★ ★ ★ ★ ★ ★ ★ ★ ★ ★ ★ ★ ★ ★

Perhaps the most important victim of the gimmick mentality is language itself. In language, the gimmick substitutes a brief phrase or slang word for a more comprehensive, clear, elaborate and proper phraseology. Compare these sample examples:

■**Gimmick:** "Everything's cool. Roddy copped the lid for a tenspot. If only he could get his hands on some snow."

□**Proper English:** "I am happy to report that all is going well. Our friend Roderick fortunately was able to purchase an ounce of marijuana for the low price of 10 dollars. It would, in addition, be agreeable if he were able to buy some cocaine."

Clearly, the wheels of commerce, not to mention the airs of discourse, are frightfully undermined by the ubiquitous gimmick (gim'ik).
► ► ► ► ► ► ► ► ► ► ► ► ►

Once the gimmick falls into common use, it creates an addiction. Gimmick-racked man becomes dependent on tricks to simplify his existence. Whole philosophies are reduced to code words. The art of thinking slowly dies out.

In the end, the proliferation of gimmicks results in a *loss of concentration*. Without *concentration,* a person requires constant exposure to EYE—GRABBING devices designed to move his sluggish mind from point A to point B.

Nowhere is this despicable trend more in evidence than in the electronic realms of television and radio. And let us not pull ★ ★ ★ ☆ ☆ ☆ **Punches.** Let's talk about news.
◄ ◄ ◄ ◄ ◄ ◄ ◄ ◄ ◄ ◄ ◄ ◄ ◄

The electronic media insist on tainting the gathering of hard news with garish injections of pop art g*mm*ckry. An example comes to mind.

A police sweep of prostitutes and their customers was reported recently by a prominent local radio station. Rather than choose simply to give their listeners the FACTS, the station embellished them by playing a recording of a song called "Bad Girls" behind the voice of the newsman.

#•/* + ‡7$.

Fortunately, with the passage of time one thing has resisted the TIDAL WAVE of g*mm*ckr: The good old-fashioned newspaper, like this one. The hallmark of the local news column has and forever will be:

- *Straight talk.*
- ✓ **No hype.**
- ☐ CLEAR THINKING.

The writing must be good enough to sustain the ATTENTION of the laziest reader. There should never be any need for special g**m*c*s to

lure

the eye.

However, it should be noted that, with the invention of the computer writing terminal, the modern newspaper writer faces a strong temptation to employ all manner of computer-generated doodads. ¶©§@ °[*Stop That!*]

In past times, it was the editor's responsibility to preserve the traditional style of a newspaper's columns and thank God for the ■EDITOR■. Of course, with the tremendous pressures of daily deadlines an occasional crack ►_____◄ will open in the smooth facade of a paper's news reporting.

To summarize: Moral man is in grave danger from a deepening addiction to g***i**s which have their origins in the invention of the wheel and have as their most enthusiastic contemporary purveyors the electronic media.

Only the printed wOrd can save us now. ✓

Veneering
Disease
afflicts us

Some of you may have come to expect human interest stories from this column. Others may expect hi-tone polemic. Still others may expect sticky drivel. Today, though, we explore the vast and troublesome realms of veneering.

Veneering is that ancient art of covering up something old with something new and nice. That is the theory of it.

The subject arises because today these offices are filled with overalled men carting desk veneers around on their shoulders and begging the pardon of persons who, until that moment, were unaware they were about to be veneered.

That is, they were to receive a new desk top composed of the standard wood-chip/fiberboard, sawdust and glue composition material with the photographic Sure-Real Wood© laminated stuff on the top. I'm sure you know what I mean.

The overall purpose of the veneering here today, we are led to believe, is a general upgrading of the facilities in anticipation of future paint work to complement the veneer.

Having received my very own veneered desk some months ago, I am in a position to view today's proceedings with some detachment. What, then, is in the nature of veneering? Let us consider three key points.

1. As stated above, veneers are called for when something is perceived as having grown old and ugly. The veneer lends a "modern" appearance to desks, buildings, human bodies, etc.

2. Veneers are almost never a genuine material of any kind. Since they are designed to cover objects, veneers have to be very thin and capable of being applied without adding measurably to the bulk of the object.

3. Veneers are calculated to draw the short-term favorable response. Having received a new desk top, the average office worker feels grateful for his "new desk."

Despite this morale boost in the short run, veneers invariably are a blight in the long run. They just don't work out. Consider building facades.

Any given town of several thousand people or more has a Main Street strip of some sort, or a town square. Typically, if the town was built 50 years or more ago, the townsfolk by now have been stricken at least once by the craving to "renovate" their strip.

What do they do? They slap a new facade on Tommy's Shoe Store. They cover over the bricks, the venerable stone and the trim of the store with some kind of modern paneling and up-to-date script lettering. Sometimes, even, a reflective veneer is called for.

For years, the townsfolk are happy as clams. But inevitably the trendy veneer, being composed of a mysterious and degradable material, begins to look pretty ratty and out-of-date. Then a new veneer is required. And another and another, until the urban renewal bulldozer comes in and mercifully kills the whole thing off.

In Kansas City, the old Southwestern Bell Telephone Building at 11th and Oak is a classic case of veneering disease. Formerly an ornate Neo-Gothic structure, the building was reworked by Alexander Barket into a "modern" white and gold-striped tower. No doubt, someone someday will decide that the building is no longer modern and will strip in a new veneer of, say, Sure-Real Granite ©.

The human body is subjected to the same cycle. We get old, we wrinkle, we're not happy with our noses, our eyelids. So with the aid of the plastic surgeon we strip in a new veneer. We update ourselves from time to time, trying to ignore the fact that everything, including ourselves, must grow old and die.

For pure grotesqueness, there is nothing that quite compares with an ancient, veneered-young Sure-Real Person ©. Not to mention what some of us look like after the mortician has veneered us up for the funeral.

All of this wouldn't be so bad' if the cult of the veneer didn't have a nasty habit of doubling back on us. Seeing all these veneers around us, we are inspired to put veneers on things even before they get old.

Take the Federal Building at 601 E. 12th. Some people think this building looks like a giant space heater, but I think it resembles a massive veneered shoe store. They only thing that's missing is the Uncle Sam's Shoes sign. But this is no veneer. The building was designed to look like that originally.

In conclusion, I think we should lighten up on the veneers in general. If we just keep the old bricks, skin and desk tops clean, they'll survive well enough.

Plain
Talk
on buying
Generic

Kansas Citians, it seems, are thinking generic. I know I am.

There was a time when I snubbed the plain-label products, though. After all, they don't look very good. Who wants to buy beer that just says "Beer" on the can, with no fancy colors, no nifty slogans, no exaggerated claims and no advertising behind it?

Most of us are accustomed to frivolous packaging features and are, at least at first, almost shocked to see consumer products without them.

Like a lot of people, I like to be told to "let it be Lowenbrau." I need to know that "it's the water" or that my "weekends were made for Michelob." I like being congratulated that I'm not drinking some "flat-land beer."

So why do the suds in my refrigerator now just say "Beer" on the front?

Fact is, I'm going generic these days — as you can see from my picture at the beginning of this chapter. A lot of us are going generic. It's cheaper.

Groceries in the area are stocking a growing variety of the plain-label products, which are made by familiar manufacturers and sold at 20 percent to 40 percent below the cost of regular-label brands. Nationally the Food Marketing Institute reports that almost 2 percent of supermarket goods are now generic.

But there's more to this generic fad than just the inexpensiveness of the products. Generic products have a kind of reverse chic about them, I think. Generic food products today are where designer jeans were a few years ago — just beginning to catch fire.

Someday, no doubt, other industries will go generic. Consumers will wear generic jeans, ride in generic automobiles, dine at generic restaurants, read generic columnists . . .

Someday people will begin to appreciate that going generic has a political side to it as well. A generic consumer makes a political statement when he puts down his dollar for a black-and-white bag of Assorted Cookies that says on the side: "These cookies may vary in size or shape. They are of good eating quality and particularly suitable for everyday use."

But what is so political about eating plain-label cookies?

Look at it this way: Using generic products can be your way of accommodating yourself to this new "Era of Limits" in which we find ourselves. As a generic consumer you can get ready for a no-frills future and be proud of it.

Generic products have that "Soviet bloc look" about them, don't you see? When an American eats generic, he's showing the world he's one Yankee capitalist who's ready to cut back a little on his gluttony. He's showing solidarity.

OK, you admit, maybe this generic columnist has got a point. But what do these black-and-white products really taste like? Are Assorted Cookies actually edible?

To which I will answer: Yes, the Assorted Cookies are adequately tasty and, like the label says, "suitable for everyday use." Of course, "assorted" may mean only two different kinds of cookies in the bag. And some people have reported that their Assorted Cookies were slightly crumbled. But, hey, who expects perfect?

In my experience, other good generic products include the Chunk Light Tuna Fish In Water, the Toothpaste, the Beer and the Orange Juice.

The Barbecue Sauce, while not quite up to Gates & Sons standards, is spicy and reasonably thick (although it looks too much like plain ketchup).

The Crunchy Peanut Butter is every bit as flavorful as Peter Pan, although it must be conceded that there are fewer chunks.

The Italian Dressing is good and suffers only mildly in comparison with Missouri-made Ott's Italian Dressing (the generic brand, distributed by Topco, goes a little heavy on the soybean oil).

Of course, there are a few disappointments.

The Chicken Pot Pie is one of them. It looks like your ordinary chicken pot pie; the label says, "Serve this product as you would any pot pie." But what the label doesn't say is that inside the crust there's precious little food. I counted 13 tiny chunks of processed chicken, seven peas and 13 fingernail-sized slices of carrot.

The Imitation Mayonnaise is another mild disappointment, with its springy consistency and strange herb taste. And, finally, the Cheese Spread Substitute is a generic Waterloo.

But you don't have to buy Cheese Spread Substitute to go generic.

No, all you have to do is try something in one of those black-and-white packages and then display it prominently in your home, so your friends will notice. They'll be impressed.

And be sure you serve your beer in the can.

Worried
sick about my
Health

I wake up in the morning. So far so good.

I fry some eggs and eat them. Eggs used to be bad for me — too much cholesterol — but now the experts say eggs may be good for me. The experts say too much cholesterol causes heart disease but too little cholesterol causes cancer of the colon. I finish my eggs, ambivalently.

They would have tasted better if I'd put more salt on them. But the experts say too much salt is not good for you (and, I'm told, too much pepper may cause hermorrhoids. So, easy on the seasonings).

I take a multivitamin because it seems like a good idea.

I resist coffee because I know too much coffee is bad for the heart and bad for the stomach and, besides, it discolors the teeth. I'm preparing for old age, knowing that someday coffee will probably really discolor my dentures.

Finishing the morning paper, I wipe the ink from my hands, concerned that some expert or other has concluded that ink isn't good for you if it gets absorbed into the bloodstream. I don't know if this is true, but I play it safe.

Stepping outside on my way to work I consider the fact that my hair is wet and it is cold outside. It seems I am very likely to catch cold. Do wetheads catch more colds than energy hogs who use hair dryers? I conclude that catching a cold is better than starting World War III because I am an energy hog.

Cranking up my car I feel momentarily guilty because the engine needs a ring job and is spewing blue smoke into the atmosphere. Blue smoke, I realize, is not good for living things. Driving down Southwest Trafficway, my car billowing smoke behind me, I keep a close watch out for other drivers. I look to the front, side and back because I know that without warning some other driver could send me to the Promised Land. I've read the statistics.

I get to work in one piece and settle down for a day of labor. The first order of business is to drink that coffee I resisted earlier. The coffee is still bad for me, but if I don't drink it now I'll fall asleep at the desk.

Falling asleep on the job is very hazardous to one's health because, as many people know, unemployment and poverty have been linked to malnutrition and other things I'm pretty sure would be bad for me.

Pouring the coffee, I briefly consider the question of sugar. To sugar or not to sugar, that is the question. Refined sugar, the experts say, is bad for you. But without it I can't stand coffee and if I can't stand coffee how am I going to service my coffee habit?

Next on the worry agenda is the matter of non-dairy creamer — that mysterious powdery stuff that looks like crushed chalk and tastes a little like cream. Intuitively, I believe the experts think very little of non-dairy creamer. Nevertheless. . . .

Drinking my coffee along with the other coffee addicts, I invariably begin to smell tobacco smoke wafting around the room. I quit smoking five years ago because it was bad for me. But now the experts are saying that just being close to a smoker may cause cancer. I consider taking up smoking again.

Lunchtime brings welcome relief. All morning long I have been experiencing job-related stress, which I read somewhere is bad for me. Lunch offers a break from this serious hazard.

Lunch also, of course, poses its own set of hazards, some of a very serious nature. According to Ralph Nader, king of the experts, I should avoid hot dogs. The vending machine food is full of preservatives deplored by other experts. Cola and other soft drinks will rot my stomach, I understand. Pies and cakes will make me fat.

Deeply worried but undeterred, I eat most of these things and hope for the best.

The afternoon passes in a blur of job-related stress, uninvited cigarette smoke, coffee, sugar, non-dairy creamer (maybe one little chocolate bar) and ink smearing off the newspaper. Occasionally, I look up at the vents in the office ceiling and wonder whether there is any asbestos floating in my air.

I pause to reflect on the miracle at work around me. Here are all these people enduring an awful reign of danger — and yet their terror is reduced to a mere furrowed brow!

My brow deeply furrowed after a long day, I wend my way home praying no truck on the interstate will flatten me. I listen to the news of the day on the radio. What was that he said? Water causes cancer?

No, I must have misunderstood. But just to be on the safe side, I worry a little anyway.

Special Thanks

Design   Frank and Lori Addington

Printing   Pepperdine Printing

Promotion   David Westbrook, Corporate Communications Group, Inc. and Cheryl Payne

Cover Photograph of Kansas City   Bruce Bandle

Help with proofreading   Gerry Brown, Greg Hurd